BA[barcode]NA
uides

Welcome to Barcelona

This opening fold-out contains a general map of Barcelona to help you visualize the six districts discussed in this guide, and four pages of valuable information, handy tips and useful addresses.

Discover Barcelona through six districts and six maps

A La Barceloneta / El Born / La Ciutat Vella

B El Raval / El Barrí Gòtic / La Ribera

C Sarrià / Pedralbes / Sants

D L'Eixample / Gràcia

E Montjuïc / Poble Sec / Sant Antoni

F Port Olímpic / Poblenou / La Dreta de l'Eixample

For each district there is a double page of addresses (restaurants – listed in ascending order of price – cafés, bars, tearooms, music venues and stores), followed by a fold-out map for the relevant area with the essential places to see (indicated on the map by a star ★). These places are by no means all that Barcelona has to offer, but to us they are unmissable. The grid-referencing system (**A** B2) makes it easy for you to pinpoint addresses quickly on the map.

Transportation and hotels in Barcelona

The last fold-out consists of a transportation map and four pages of practical information that include a selection of hotels.

Thematic index

Lists all the street names, sites and addresses featured in this guide.

DISTRICTS OF BARCELONA

August
Festa major de Gràcia
→ *Around Aug 15*
Street decorations, parties and concerts in the Gràcia district.

September
Festa de la Mercè
→ *Week of the 24th*
Celebrates the patron saint of Barcelona; processions by the city's 'giants' and *capgrossos* (big heads), *castellers*, *correfocs* (fire-spitting dragons).

November-December
Festival internacional de jazz
Jazz greats perform around the city, including at the Palau de la Música (**B** B2).

OPENING TIMES

Stores
→ *Usually Mon-Sat 10am–8.30pm (10pm for department stores). Many shops still close at lunchtime (2–4.30pm). Some close Mon morning*

Museums
→ *Usually Tue-Sat 10am–7pm; Sun 10am–2pm*

Meals
Breakfast: not too early, between 9 and 11am.
Lunch (*dinars* in Catalan): around 2pm, seldom earlier. The city becomes quiet between 2 and 4pm.
Dinner (*sopars* in Catalan): also eaten late: never before 9.30pm or 10pm. Some restaurants hold two sittings: one around 8pm for tourists, and the other around 10pm for locals.

Going out
Bars close at 3am, night-clubs open 11.30pm–5am.

EATING OUT

August closure
Many establishments will be closed most of that month.

Catalan food
Based on mostly ordinary, but fresh, high-quality ingredients beautifully cooked with garlic, herbs and a good olive oil, the success of Catalan cuisine is in its simplicity.

Tapas bars
Tapas (appetizers) are perfect for small appetites (but not necessarily for small budgets). They can be eaten throughout the day. Full portion (*ración*) or half-portion (*media ración*).

Restaurants
Sandwiches (*entrepans* in Catalan, *bocadillos* in Castilian) and cheap dishes (*plats combinats*) of meat or fish, with rice or French fries are served in small eating places. Paella (a saffron-spiced meat and seafood rice dish) is usually on the menu on Thursdays. More traditional restaurants serve creative Mediterranean cuisine in comfortable surroundings. Expect a 30- to 50-minute wait in the more fashionable establishments.

MODERNIST BARCELONA

The end of the 19th century brings a new style of decoration (floral motifs, sinuous lines), supported by new materials such as laminated iron, industrial glass and concrete. The 'Block of Discord' (**D** B6) brings together three major figures:

Antoni Gaudí (1852–1926)
The most creative of the three: organic forms, rounded arches...; Sagrada Família (**D** D6).

Lluis Domènech i Montaner (1850–1923)
Imaginative decorations (stained glass, mosaics) and Catalan symbolism (mythological friezes); Palau de la Música Catalana (**B** D2).

Josep Puig i Cadafalch (1867–1956)
Inspired by Gothic and Flemish architecture, as well as medieval Catalonia; Palau Baró de Quadras (**D** B5).

Ruta del Modernismo
→ *Tickets on sale from the underground tourist office, Pl. Catalunya, 17*
Tel. 93 285 38 34

CONTEMPORARY BARCELONA

Spurred on by the 2004 Forum of Cultures, Barcelona has acquired a futuristic skyline.

Torre Agbar (**F** C2)
→ *Plaça de les Glòries*
Concrete and glass tower (466 ft) by Jean Nouvel.

Edifici Fòrum (off **F** D3)
→ *Passeig de García Fària*
Astonishing blue triangle in suspension, by Herzog and De Meuron.

FAÇADE IN POBLENOU

CITY PROFILE

- 1.8 million inhabitants
- Surface area of 37.8 square miles
- 16 districts
- Capital of Catalonia and Spain's second capital after Madrid
- 24 percent of Spanish people speak Catalan

STREET IN THE BARRI GÒTIC

CATALAN WORDS

Bon dia, bona tarde, bona nit: Good morning good afternoon, good night
Adéu: Goodbye
Si us plau: Please
Gràcies: Thank you
¿Com està? How are you?
Molt bé: Very well
¿Quant val?: How much is it?
¿Quina hora és? What time is it?
Son les... : It's...
Voldria... : I'd like...
Pot indicar-me on és... : Can you tell me where...
A prop, lluny: Near, far
A la dreta, a l'esquerra: Right, left

TOURIST INFO

Tourist switchboard
→ *Tel. 93 285 38 34*
Mon-Sat 9am–8pm
Tourist offices
Plaça de Catalunya (**B** C2)
→ *Plaça de Catalunya, 17 (underground)*
Daily 9am–9pm
Plaça Sant Jaume (**B** C4)
→ *Carrer de la Ciutat, 2*
Mon-Fri 9am–8pm; Sat 10am–8pm; Sun 10am–2pm
Estació de Sants (**C** B5)
→ *Mon-Fri 8am–8pm; Sat-Sun 8am–2pm (8pm summer)*

WWW.

→ *gencat.net*
Generalitat of Catalunya's official website.
→ *barcelonaturisme.com*
The comprehensive official website of the tourist office.
→ *bcn.es*
→ *bcn-guide.com*
→ *barcelona-on-line.es*

Internet cafés
Internet Café (**A** D1)
→ *Carrer Barra de Ferro, 3*
Daily 10am (noon Sat-Sun)–10pm
Ovni (**B** D4)
→ *Via Laietana, 32*
Daily 9am–midnight
30 free minutes with drink.
Easy Internet Café (**B** C2)
→ *Ronda de la Universitat, 35 or rambla Capuxtins, 31*
Daily 8am–2.30am

TELEPHONE

USA / UK to Barcelona
→ *011 (from the US) or 00 (from the UK) + 34 (Spain) + nine-digit number*
Barcelona to USA / UK
→ *00 + 1 (USA) or + 44 (UK) + number*
Useful numbers
Police: 091 or 092
Fire service: 080
Emergencies: 112
24-hour pharmacies: 93 481 00 60
Information: 010

DIARY OF EVENTS

January
Cabalgata de los Reyes Magos
→ *Jan 5, Epiphany eve,*
Arrival of the Three Kings in the harbor; distribution of sweets to the children.
February
Carnestoltes (Carnival)
→ *Shrove Tuesday*
Carnival procession down the Rambles.
Festa de Santa Eulàlia
→ *Around Feb 12*
Celebrates the former patron saint of Barcelona. Concerts and *castellers* (human pyramids) in the Ciutat Vella (Barri Gòtic, El Raval and La Ribera).
April-June
Festa de Sant Jordi
→ *April 23*
Patron saint of Catalonia. Lovers exchange books and roses. Book and flower stalls down the Rambles and on Plaça Sant Jaume are decorated.
Festival de música antiga
→ *April-May*
Open-air concerts of ancient music in the Barri Gòtic and at the Caixa Fòrum center.
Festival de guitarra
→ *April-June*
Classical, jazz, and flamenco guitar.
June
Sónar
→ *Three days in June*
International festival of electronic music has the CCCB Museum (**B** B2) as its headquarters.
Festa de Sant Joan
→ *Night of the 23rd*
Also called the Nit del Foc (night of fire). Fireworks and bonfires on the beaches.
July
Festa del Grec
The city's most important summer cultural festival: theater, dance, music in the Montjuïc Greek theater.

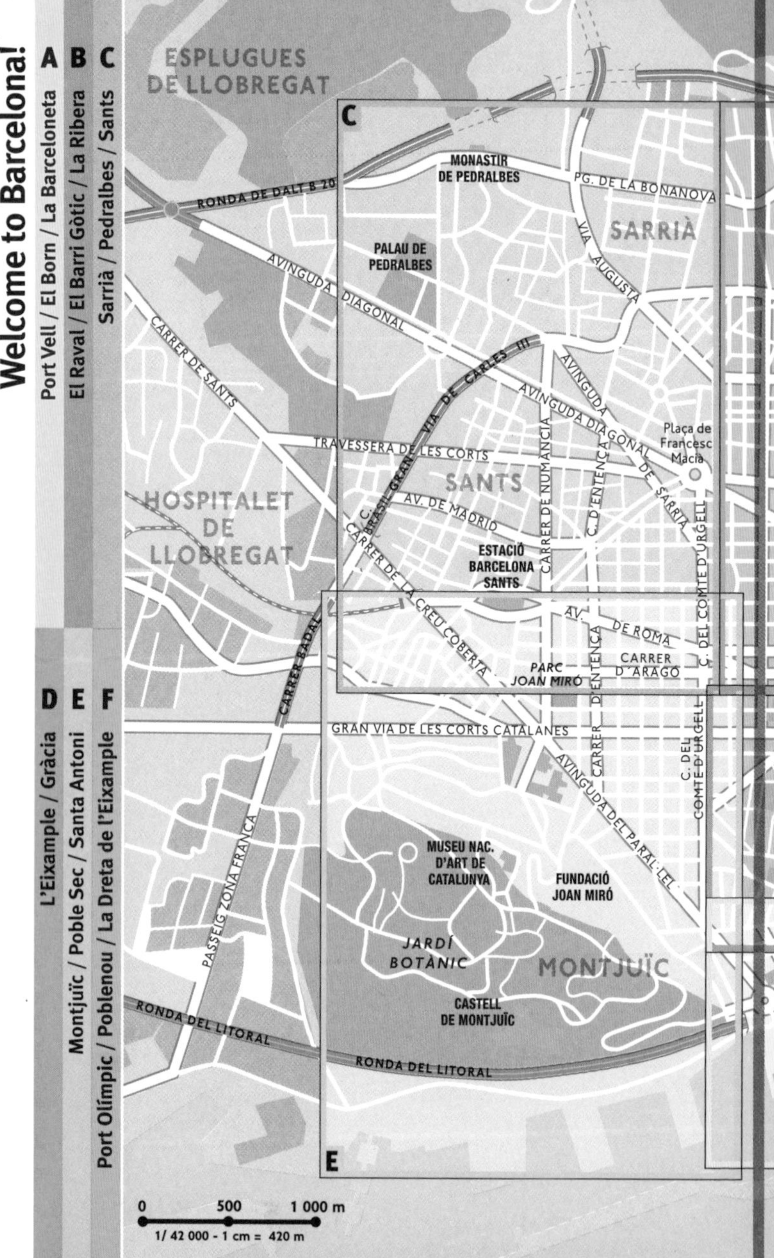
Welcome to Barcelona!
A B C
Port Vell / El Born / La Barceloneta
El Raval / El Barri Gòtic / La Ribera
Sarrià / Pedralbes / Sants
D E F
L'Eixample / Gràcia
Montjuïc / Poble Sec / Santa Antoni
Port Olímpic / Poblenou / La Dreta de l'Eixample
ESPLUGUES DE LLOBREGAT
C
MONASTIR DE PEDRALBES
RONDA DE DALT B 20
PG. DE LA BONANOVA
SARRIÀ
VIA AUGUSTA
PALAU DE PEDRALBES
AVINGUDA DIAGONAL
CARRER DE SANTS
GRAN VIA DE CARLES III
AVINGUDA
AVINGUDA DIAGONAL
Plaça de Francesc Macià
TRAVESSERA DE LES CORTS
SANTS
DE SARRIÀ
HOSPITALET DE LLOBREGAT
C. BRASIL
AV. DE MADRID
CARRER DE NUMÀNCIA
C. D'ENTENÇA
CARRER DE LA CREU COBERTA
ESTACIÓ BARCELONA SANTS
C. DEL COMTE D'URGELL
AV. DE ROMA
CARRER BADAL
CARRER D'ARAGÓ
PARC JOAN MIRÓ
CARRER D'ENTENÇA
GRAN VIA DE LES CORTS CATALANES
C. DEL COMTE D'URGELL
AVINGUDA DEL PARAL·LEL
MUSEU NAC. D'ART DE CATALUNYA
FUNDACIÓ JOAN MIRÓ
PASSEIG ZONA FRANCA
JARDÍ BOTÀNIC
MONTJUÏC
CASTELL DE MONTJUÏC
RONDA DEL LITORAL
RONDA DEL LITORAL
E
0
500
1 000 m
1/ 42 000 - 1 cm = 420 m

A

Port Vell / El Born / La Barceloneta

To the south of El Born, from Port Vell to La Barceloneta, the salty tang in the air is a constant reminder of the nearby sea. The capital of Catalonia has been revamping its waterfront since the 1992 Olympics and gradually renovating the old neighborhoods. El Born, now a place to be seen for the city's fashion-conscious inhabitants, contains some medieval gems that have been restored and converted into museums and art galleries, while all over La Barceloneta (Little Barcelona), you find evidence of the city's rich seafaring and fishing heritage, which has diminished but is far from forgotten.

The à la carte prices given in this guide are average prices for a two-course meal with one drink.

LES QUINZE NITS

EL XAMPANYET

RESTAURANTS

Les Quinze Nits (**A** C1)
→ *Plaça Reial, 6*
Tel. 93 317 30 75; Daily 1–3.30pm, 8.30–11.30pm
The elaborate but reasonably priced Italian-style cuisine explains the success of this restaurant, under the arcades of Plaça Reial, and every day a queue starts forming outside its doors long before opening time. If you are too impatient or hungry to stand in line, go next door to Taxidermista, at no. 8. Set lunch €9.

Senyor Parellada (**A** D1)
→ *Carrer de l'Argenteria, 37*
Tel. 93 310 50 94; Daily 1–3.30pm, 8.30–11.30pm
The consistently delicious Catalan dishes of the day have won this restaurant its good reputation. They are are served in a pretty setting, spread over two levels, around a glass-covered courtyard.
Carte €25.

Cal Pep (**A** E1)
→ *Plaça de les Olles, 8*
Tel. 93 310 79 61; Mon 8–11.30pm; Tue-Sat 1–4pm, 8pm–midnight (1am Fri-Sat)
Cal Pep presides at the bar, where an eager line of regulars enjoy tapas such as fried baby cuttlefish, gambas *a la planxa*, clams and baby peppers. Wait, a chilled white wine in hand, in hope that a place at the bar becomes free before too long. Carte €25.

Salero (**A** E1)
→ *Carrer del Rec, 60*
Tel. 93 319 80 22; Daily 1.30–4pm, 9pm–midnight (1am Fri-Sat); closed Sun lunch
It has a minimalist decor with gentle colors and lighting, fresh flowers and soft background music. The regularly changing menu uses Mediterranean ingredients to produce unusual local and foreign dishes, always with very fresh fish. Set lunch €12; carte €30.

Set Portes (**A** D1)
→ *Passeig d'Isabel II, 14*
Tel. 93 319 30 33
Daily 1pm–1am
In business since 1836. You will meet here an equal number of tourists and locals. The paella and the *escalivada* are always a good bet. Fast, efficient service. Carte €50–70.

Cal Pinxo (**A** D2)
→ *Plaça de Pau Vila*
Tel. 93 221 21 11; Daily noon–4pm, 7.30–11.30pm
A seafood restaurant by the Museu d'Història, with a view of the marina. Inside or out on the veranda, enjoy excellent

Map B →

↑ Map E

PLAÇA REIAL

PALAU GÜELL

LES RAMBLES

A
B
C
1
2
3

EL RAVAL
BARRI G
PORT VELL

CARRER DE SANT PAU
CARRER DEL MARQUÈS DE BARBERÀ
C. DE ST. OLEGUER
C. DE LES PENEDIDES
C. DE LA UNIÓ
RBLA. DELS CAPUTXINS
CARRER DE FERRAN
Plaça de Sant Jaum
AJUNT
Plaça de Sant Miquel
CARRER
C. DE LA CIUTAT
MONESTIR DE SANT PAU DEL CAMP
PLAÇA REIAL
C. NOU DE ZURBANO
C. DE VIDRE
C. DE LES TÀPIES
CARRER NOU DE LA RAMBLA
PALAU GÜELL
C. DE L'EST
C. DE GUÀRDIA
Plaça de la Verónica
C. DE REGOMIR
C. DELS ESCUDELLERS
AVINGUDA DEL PARAL·LEL
AVINGUDA DE LES DRASSANES
C. DE STA. MADRONA
CARRER DE L'OM
L'ARC DEL TEATRE
RAMBLA DE STA. MÒNICA
Plaça del Teatre
C. NOU DE ST. FRANCESC
CARRER OBRADORS
C. DELS CÒDOLS
C. D'EN CARABASSA
C. D'EN SERRA
D'AVINYÓ
C. D'ATAÜLF
C. D'EN C
C. DE STA. MÒNICA
C. DE MONTSERRAT
CARRER DE
JARDINS DE LES TRES XEMENEIES
C. DEL CID
LES RAMBLES
CARRER AM
LA MERCÈ
C. DE SILS
MUSEU DE CERA
CARRER DE PALAUDÀRIES
C. DE PORTAL DE STA. MADRONA
DRASSANES
CARRER DE J. ANSELM CLAVÉ
Plaça de la Mercé
CAPITANIA GENERAL
JARDINS DEL BALUARD
Plaça del Duc de Medinaceli
PG. DE C
CARRER PUIG I XORIGUER
MUSEU MARÍTIM
Plaça Portal de la Pau
PASSEIG DE COLOM
C. DE VILA I VILÀ
ST. PERE CLAVER
LITORA
C. DE CARRERA
RONDA DEL
JARDINS DE W. BENJAMIN
CARNER
Moll de Bosch i Alsina
Plaça de les Drassanes
DUANES
MONUMENT A COLOM
PG. DE JOSEP
DÀRSENA NACIONAL
Moll de les Drassanes
RAMBLA DE MAR
RONDA DEL LITORAL
IMAX
Moll de Sant Bertran
Moll de Barcelona
AQUÀRIU
MAREMÀGNUM
Moll d'Espanya
TORRE DE JAUME I
PORT VELL
DÀRSENA DE SANT BERTRÀN
ESTACIÓ

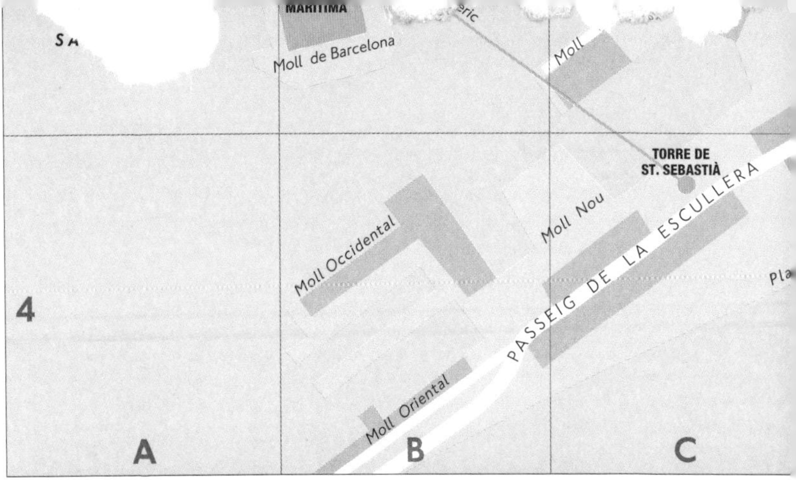

MARITIMA

Moll de Barcelona

Moll

TORRE DE
ST. SEBASTIÀ

Moll Nou

Moll Occidental

PASSEIG DE LA ESCULLERA

Pla

4

Moll Oriental

A

B

C

METRÒNOM

MERCAT DEL BORN

MUSEU MARÍTIM

★ **Plaça Reial** (**A** C1)
Built between 1848 and 1859, this is one of Barcelona's busiest squares. Plaça Reial is the only square in the city to be designed as a set piece and there is an extraordinary architectural unity as a result. The shady palm trees and the street lamps (designed by the young Antonio Gaudí in 1878) which surround the Three Graces fountain help to soften the austere lines of the square's buildings. There are many stores, bars and *cervecerías* (brasseries) under the arcades and covered passageways leading off the square.

★ **Palau Güell** (**A** B1)
→ *Carrer Nou de la Rambla, 3*
Tel. 93 317 39 74
Tue-Sat 10am–2.30pm
The first work to be commissioned by Count Güell, an enlightened patron of the arts. All the hallmarks of Gaudí's genius are united here. From the ground floor to the chimneys the master juggled proportions and materials (iron, wood and mosaics) and played with color to produce what was his first major work (1889).

★ **Les Rambles** (**A** B1)
There is a stunning view over the Rambles (Ramblas in Castilian) from the cable car linking La Barceloneta to Montjuïc. Built on a riverbed which formed the western boundary of the city until it dried up in the 18th century, the Rambles is now a splendid and lively street running from the Plaça de Catalunya down to the seafront.

★ **Museu Picasso** (**A** E1)
→ *Carrer Montcada, 15–23*
Tel. 93 256 30 00
Tue-Sun 10am–8pm;
www.museupicasso.bcn.es
The largest collection of the master's early works (1895–1904), displaying his remarkable technique and academic training. The museum occupies five elegant palaces in Carrer Montcada, which was a bourgeois street from the 15th to the 18th century. I 2008 new rooms opened which will be dedicated t changing exhibit of some 1,500 of Picasso's prints, engravings and lithograp

★ **Santa Maria del Mar** (**A** D1)
→ *Plaça de Santa Maria*
Tel. 93 310 23 90; Daily 9am–1.30pm, 4.30–7pm
The best example of Catalan Gothic architectu Built in only 55 years (1329–84), the basilica has an incredible harmor The delicacy of the pillars supporting the three nave creates a good sense of space. The acoustics are exceptional.

EXCURSIONS

THE BEACHES

A few minutes from the center of Barcelona, 2 ½ miles of beaches easily accessible by public transportatio
Platja del Bogatell, P de La Mar Bella (F D
→ *Subway Barcelon Ciutadella-Vila Olím Bogatell or Llacun bus nos 36, 40, 41,*
Perfectly equippec (showers and endl restaurants), this pa is ideal for cyclists, skaters and joggers
Information
→ *Tel. 93 481 00 5 (info on the temperat the air, the water, the strength of the wind e*

Specialties

A la planxa/a la brasa: grilled. **Arròs amb conill:** rabbit with rice. **Arròs negre:** black rice with squid ink.
Botifarra amb mongetes: black sausage cooked in white wine and served with haricot beans.
Canelons d'espinacs: spinach cannelloni.
Cava: Catalan champagne.
Crema catalana: caramel flan. **Embotits:** assorted sausages. **Escalivada:** grilled peppers and eggplant, seasoned nd dressed with olive oil.
Escudella i carn d'olla: meat and vegetable broth, a Catalan Christmas dish
Espinacs a la catalana: spinach with pine nuts and raisins. **Faves a la catalana:** broad beans, onions and botifarra. **Mel i mató:** cottage cheese with honey.
Pà amb tomaquet: slice of bread rubbed with fresh tomato and oil.
Truites: Spanish omelets made with egg and potato and available with a variety of ingredients.

Tipping

Service is usually included, but you can round up the bill (5–10 percent).

SHOWS

Reservations

FNAC (B C2)
→ *Plaça de Catalunya, 4*
Tel. 93 344 18 00
Mon-Sat 10am–10pm
Servicaixa
→ *Tel. 902 33 22 11*
Daily 8am–8pm
Also at La Caixa banks ATMs.

Discounts

Tiquet–3 (B C2)
→ *Plaça de Catalunya, 17*
Tel. 902 10 12 12
Half-price seats, available three hours before each performance.

Programs

Go BCN
→ *Free monthly (in music shops, clubs, bars)*
What's hip in Barcelona, plus a diary of concerts throughout the country.
Butxaca
→ *Free monthly (in bars, FNAC)*
Listings of cultural events (concerts, movies, exhibitions, etc.).
Guía del Ocio
→ *Every Thu; €1*
Complete listings: movies, theater, concerts, etc.

GOING OUT

Around midnight visit the bars in the Barrí Gòtic or El Born. then head for a club in the Poble Espanyol or in L'Eixample. Round the night off around 6am in one of the area's *afterhours*.

Gay Barcelona

Barcelona is one of the most tolerant and open-minded cities in Europe, known for its vibrant, integrated gay scene. Centrally located gay bars, clubs, and hotels abound, many in L'Eixa but also in El Raval, El Gràcia, and Montjuic.

MUSEUMS

Reduced-price tickets

Mainly for over-65s, under-12s and students.
Articket
→ *Available from participating museums, by phone (Tel. Entrada, 902 10 12 12), or at Caixa Catalunya banks; €17*
Free entry to MACBA (**B** B2), CCCB (**B** B2), Fundació Antoni Tàpies (**D** B6), La Pedrera (**D** B5), MNAC (**E** B3), and Fundació Joan Miró (**E** C4).

SHOPPING

Shopping streets

Avinguda Diagonal
From Passeig de Gràcia to Plaça de Francesc Macià some of the top names in fashion design (Armani, Calvin Klein etc.).

THE SEA IS NEVER FAR AWAY

SIGHTSEEING BY CABLE CAR

VIEW FROM THE TIBIDABO

Passeig de Gràcia and Rambla de Catalunya
International and Spanish fashion (Zara, Mango, Camper), perfumes.
Portal de l'Àngel
Pedestrian street. Prêt-à-porter, shoes, lingerie.
Carrer de Portaferrissa
Young casual wear, jewelry, accessories.
Carrer de la Riera Baixa
A clubber's paradise. Piercing, tattooing.
Carrer d'Avinyó
Designers' street: fashion wear and accessories.

Department stores and shopping centers

El Corte Inglès (**B** C2)
→ *Plaça de Catalunya, 14*
Several branches.
See also **C**.
Diagonal Mar (off map)
→ *Av. Diagonal, 3; Fòrum or El Maresme subway stations*
A shopping center by the sea.
Les Glòries (**F** D2)
→ *Av. Diagonal, 208*
More than 200 stores.
Maremàgnum (**A** C3)
→ *Moll d'Espanya*
A shopping center right on the seafront, open daily until 11pm.

Sales

Twice a year: mid-Jan-end Feb and July-Aug.

Covered markets

La Boquería, or Mercat de Sant Josep (**B** B3)
→ *La Rambla, 91; Mon-Fri 8am–8.30pm; Sat 8am–8pm*
One of Europe's finest fruit and vegetable markets.
Mercat de Sant Antoni (**E** D3)
→ *Carrer d. Comte d'Urgell, 1 Mon-Sat 7am–2.30pm, 5.30–8.30pm (no interruption Fri)*
Mercat de la Concepció (**D** C6)
→ *Carrer d'Aragó, 313 Mon-Sat 8am–8pm (3pm Mon; 4pm Sat)*
Mercat de la Barceloneta (**A** E3)
→ *Plaça de la Font, 12; Mon-Sat 7am–2pm (3pm Sat)*

BARCELONA ANOTHER WAY

On foot

→ *Daily 10am and Tue-Sun 10.30am; Fri-Sat 11am–4pm in summer; Sat 11.30am–noon; €9–11*
Guided tours in English or Castilian around the Barri Gòtic. Departure from the tourist office in Plaça de Catalunya.

By boat

Golondrinas (**A** B2)
→ *Plaça Portal de la Pau Tel. 93 442 31 06; Daily 11.30am–6pm (7pm summer)*
Scenic ferry trips around the harbor.

By cable car

Transbordador Aeri (**A** C4)
→ *From torre de Sant Sebastià (Barceloneta) to Estació Miramar (Montjuïc) Tel. 93 441 48 20; Daily 10.45am–7pm (8pm June-Oct); €12.50 return*
Dizzying views of the bay. Not for the fainthearted!

EXCURSIONS

Costa Brava

North of Barcelona, 125 miles of rugged coastline.
Cadaqués / Cap de Creus
→ *By Sarfa bus from Barcelona-Estació del Nord*
Lovely fishing village with whitewashed houses. Superb view from the Cap de Creus lighthouse.

Costa Dorada

The Catalan riviera.
Sitges
→ *By train from Estació de Sants*
Lively seaside resort. Famous carnival and movie festival (Nov).
Tarragona
→ *By train from Estació de Sants*
UNESCO-listed for its unique Roman vestiges. Interesting medieval quarter.

Inland

Girona
→ *By train from Estació de Sants*
Charming historical town with flower-laden streets. Medieval Jewish quarter, Gothic cathedral and city walls.
Figueres
→ *By train from Estació de Sants*
Dalí's native town. Its unusual theater, converted by the artist himself into the Teatre-Museu Dalí, attracts many visitors.
Montserrat
→ *Coaches from Estació de Sants or the R5 Line train from Plaça d'Espanya station, then the 'Cremallera'*
Centuries-old Benedictine monastery perched in unusual-looking mountains. Walking paths.

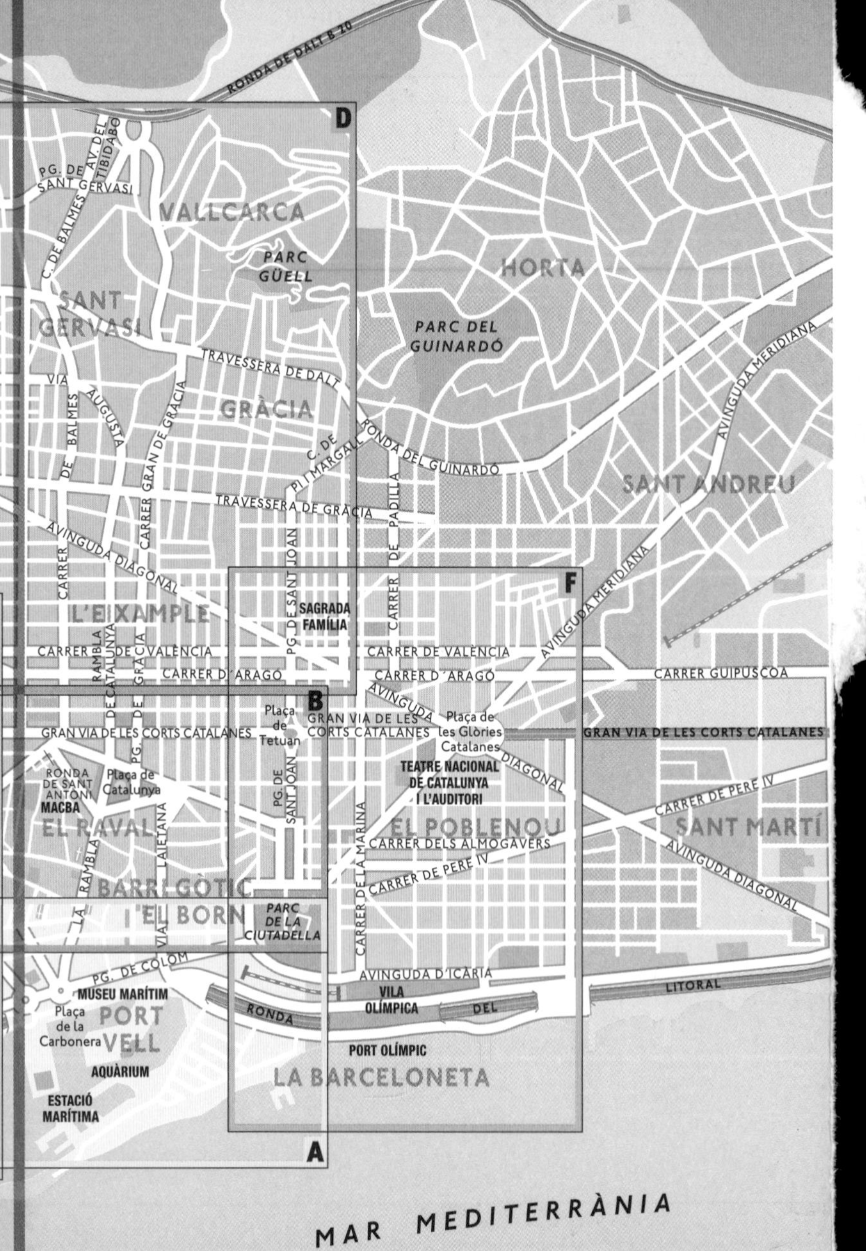
RONDA DE DALT B 20
D
PG. DE SANT GERVASI
AV. DEL TIBIDABO
C. DE BALMES
VALLCARCA
PARC GÜELL
HORTA
SANT GERVASI
PARC DEL GUINARDÓ
TRAVESSERA DE DALT
VIA AUGUSTA
CARRER DE BALMES
CARRER GRAN DE GRÀCIA
GRÀCIA
AVINGUDA MERIDIANA
C. DE PI I MARGALL
RONDA DEL GUINARDÓ
SANT ANDREU
TRAVESSERA DE GRÀCIA
CARRER DE PADILLA
PG. DE SANT JOAN
AVINGUDA DIAGONAL
CARRER
F
L'EIXAMPLE
SAGRADA FAMÍLIA
AVINGUDA MERIDIANA
CARRER DE VALÈNCIA
CARRER DE VALÈNCIA
RAMBLA DE CATALUNYA
PG. DE GRÀCIA
CARRER D'ARAGÓ
CARRER D'ARAGÓ
CARRER GUIPÚSCOA
B
AVINGUDA
Plaça de Tetuan
GRAN VIA DE LES CORTS CATALANES
Plaça de les Glòries Catalanes
GRAN VIA DE LES CORTS CATALANES
GRAN VIA DE LES CORTS CATALANES
RONDA DE SANT ANTONI
Plaça de Catalunya
DIAGONAL
TEATRE NACIONAL DE CATALUNYA I L'AUDITORI
MACBA
PG. DE SANT JOAN
CARRER DE PERE IV
EL RAVAL
VIA LAIETANA
EL POBLENOU
SANT MARTÍ
CARRER DELS ALMOGÀVERS
LA RAMBLA
CARRER DE LA MARINA
CARRER DE PERE IV
AVINGUDA DIAGONAL
BARRI GÒTIC
EL BORN
PARC DE LA CIUTADELLA
PG. DE COLOM
AVINGUDA D'ICÀRIA
LITORAL
MUSEU MARÍTIM
VILA OLÍMPICA
Plaça de la Carbonera
PORT VELL
RONDA
DEL
PORT OLÍMPIC
AQUÀRIUM
LA BARCELONETA
ESTACIÓ MARÍTIMA
A
MAR MEDITERRÀNIA

GUIRI

ESPAI BARROC

LA PELÚ

Catalan specialties made with seasonal, extra fresh ingredients: pasta cooked in shellfish stock, razor clams, 'zarzuela'. Try the Pinxo monkfish or the parrillada (grilled seafood mixture). Carte €45–65.

CAFÉS, TAPAS

La Vinya del Senyor (**A** D1)
→ *Carrer Santa Maria, 5*
Tue-Thu noon–1am; Fri-Sun noon–2am
The terrace of this traditional bodega spills out onto the plaza of the Basilica Santa Maria del Mar. Selected wines and sherries, along with tasty, good quality ham and cheese tapas dishes.

El Xampanyet (**A** D1)
→ *Carrer de Montcada, 22*
Tel. 93 319 70 03; Tue-Sat noon–4pm, 6.30–11.30pm; Sun noon–4pm
The coolest bodega in the city has been in the Esteve family for generations. People come here for the tasty tapas, the anchovies (prepared to a secret recipe of the house), and the cider and chilled cava.

Tèxtil Cafè (**A** D1)
→ *Carrer de Montcada, 12*
Tel. 93 268 25 98
Tue-Sun 10am–midnight (1am Fri-Sat)
Located in a splendid medieval palace, which also houses the Textile Museum, this café opens onto a gorgeous Gothic patio terrace. Perfect for breakfast or a light lunch.

BARS, CLUBS

Daguiri (**A** E3)
→ *Carrer de Grau i Torras, 59*
Tel. 93 221 51 09; Daily 10am–midnight (1am Fri-Sat)
You could spend all day here: mornings reading the paper with a coffee; afternoons, after the beach, for a cool beer and a meal on the terrace facing the sea; and evenings for the cheerful atmosphere and lively music (from hip-hop to flamenco).

Suborn (**A** E1)
→ *Carrer de la Ribera, 18*
Tel. 93 310 11 10
Wed-Sat 8.30pm–3am
A former local bar, that has been transformed into a club where you can lunch (dishes are prepared using market produce), dine (a more imaginative menu) to the sound of techno music. Pleasant terrace under the arches of Passeig Picasso.

Bar Pastís (**A** B1)
→ *Carrer Santa Mònica, 4*
Tel. 93 318 79 80; Tue-Sun 7.30pm–2am (3am Fri-Sat)
You'll only find two tables and eight stools in this tiny space offering flowing pastis (aniseed-flavored aperitif) and French music. For over 50 years this has been the best place for a taste of Marseilles in the Catalan capital.

Espai Barroc (**A** D1)
→ *Carrer Montcada, 20*
Tel. 93 310 06 73; Tue-Sat 8pm–2am; Sun 6–9pm
A very unusual place in the courtyard of the Gothic Palau Dalmases, for lovers of all things elegant and cultural. The best days are Thursdays, when operatic arias are sung live, and Tuesdays for flamenco.

Astin (**A** D1)
→ *Carrer Abaixadors, 9*
Tel. 93 301 00 90
Thu-Sat 6pm–3.30am
Nitsaclub's (**E** D4) little brother. A great place for a drink while listening to today's best Spanish DJs (11pm onward).

Jamboree (**A** C1)
→ *Plaça Reial, 17; Tel. 933 19 17 89; Daily 9pm–5am*
A pioneering jazz club where legendary figures such as Chet Baker and Joshua Redman have played. At 12.30am the live music gives way to DJs spinning funk and r'n'b. Admission €9 (no drink included).

SHOPPING

La Manual Alpargatera (**A** C1)
→ *Carrer d'Avinyó, 7*
Tel. 93 301 01 72; Mon-Sat 9.30am–1.30pm, 4.30–8pm
Handmade espadrilles or Catalan version *espadenya* (with ribbons around the ankle) in every color and style, from traditional to the truly outlandish.

Casa Gispert (**A** D1)
→ *Carrer dels Sombrerers, 23*
Tue-Fri 10am–1pm, 4–7.30pm; Sat 10am–2pm, 5–8pm; closed Mon in Jan-Sep
Coffee, dried fruit, cocoa, spices, all prepared in-house since 1851.

La Pelú (**A** D1)
→ *Carrer de l'Argenteria, 70*
Tel. 93 310 48 07; Thu-Sat 10.30am (11am Sat)–9pm
The latest hairstyles by Barcelona's most creative hairdressers. Several salons in town.

Papa Bubble (**A** C1)
→ *Carrer Ample, 28; Tue-Fri 10am–2pm, 4–8.30pm; Sat 10am–8.30pm (11am Sun)*
Candies made according to traditional methods, but still popular with the younger generations.

MUSEU PICASSO

BASÍLICA SANTA MARIA DEL MAR

D
E
F
1
2
← Map B
↑ Map F

EL BORN
LA BARCELONETA
MUSEU PICASSO
MUSEU TÈXTIL
MUSEU ART PRECOLOMBÍ
GAL. MAEGHT
METRÒNOM
MERCAT DEL BORN
SANTA MARIA DEL MAR
MUSEU DE ZOOLOGIA
MUSEU DE GEOLOGIA
PARC DE LA CIUTADELLA
MUSEU D'ART MODERN
PARC ZOOLÒGIC
CORREUS
LA LLOTJA
DELEGACIÓ DEL GOVERN
ESTACIÓ DE FRANÇA
PALAU DE MAR
MUSEU D'HISTÒRIA DE CATALUNYA
MARINA
LA BARCELONETA
HOSPITAL DEL MAR
PARC DE LA BARCELONETA

Plaça de l'Àngel
Plaça de Santa Maria
Plaça de les Olles
Plaça de Palau
Plaça Comercial
Plaça d'Antonio López
Plaça de Pau Vila
Plaça de la Font
Plaça de la Barceloneta
Plaça del Poeta Boscà
Plaça de Pompeu Gener
Moll del Dipòsit
Moll de la Barceloneta

JAUME I
BARCELONETA

C. DE LA PRINCESA
C. B. DE FERRO
C. DEL VIGATANS
C. DE GRUNYÍ
CARRER DE MONTCADA
C. DE L'ARGENTERIA
C. DE BASEA
C. DELS SOMBRERERS
PG. DEL BORN
C. DE STA. MARIA
C. CANVIS NOUS
C. D'ÀNGEL J. BAIXERAS
C. DE AGULLERS
C. DEL CONSOLAT DE MAR
C. CANVIS VELLS
CARRER L'ESPASERIA
C. DE L'ESPARTERIA
C. RERA PALAU
C. DEL COMERÇ
REC
CARRER DE LA FUSINA
C. DE LA RIBERA
C. ANTIC DE SANT JOAN
C. DEL
C. D'OCATA
C. DEL GEN. CASTAÑOS
C. DE LA MARQUESA
C. DE LA RENA CRISTINA
C. DEL LLAUDER
C. DE LA FUSTERIA
VIA LAIETANA
PG. D'ISABEL II
AVINGUDA MARQUÈS DE L'ARGENTERA
PASSEIG DE PICASSO
PASSEIG DE CIRCUMVAL·LACIÓ
CARRER DEL DOCTOR AIGUADER
C. DEL DOCTOR AIGUADER
RONDA DEL LITORAL
CARRER DE BALBOA
CARRER DE GINEBRA
C. DELS PINZÓN
C. DE L'ATLÀNTIDA
C. DE BALUARD
CARRER DE SANT MIQUEL
CARRER DEL MAR
C. DE LA MAQUINISTA
PAPASSEIT
PASSEIG DE SALVAT
PASSEIG JOAN DE BORBÓ
CARRER D'ANDREA

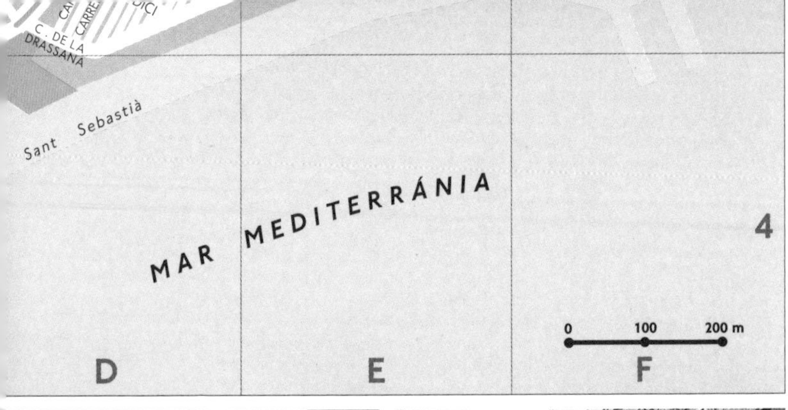

UÀRIUM

LA BARCELONETA

Metronóm (**A** E1)
Carrer de la Fusina, 9
. 93 268 42 98; Sep-July:
:-Sat 10am–2pm, 4.30–
n; closed for renovations
;ood venue for
ernative artistic events.
der the Art Deco-style
me you will find
otography exhibitions,
ıltimedia installations,
perimental music, art
d video.

Mercat del Born (**A** E1)
Plaça Comercial, 12
e huge deserted market-
ll, which housed the
gest market in Barcelona
til 1971, is one of the
est examples of 19th-
ıtury Spanish metal-
d-glass architecture.
A cultural center devoted to medieval Barcelona is being built inside (although works have been going on for a few years now), where the exceptional archeological vestiges from the 14th to the 18th century uncovered in the market-hall's basement will be displayed. These will include parts of the old district as it was before being pulled down in 1714 to allow the nearby military tower to go up.

★ **Museu Marítim** (**A** B2) / **Monument a Colom** (**A** B2)
→ *Avinguda de les Drassanes*
Tel. 93 432 99 20
Daily 10am–8pm
At the foot of Les Rambles stands the statue of Columbus (1888) pointing out to sea, paying homage to the famous explorer who, on his return from the New World, came here to present himself to the Spanish sovereign. Right by it is the Drassanes, the 13th-century medieval shipyards, miraculously preserved and converted into a maritime museum. There is a unique collection of model vessels, maps and a 16th-century Royal Galley.

★ **Aquàrium** (**A** C3)
→ *Moll d'Espanya, 7 Port Vell;*
Tel. 93 221 74 74; Daily
9.30am–9pm (11pm July-Aug)
The largest aquarium in Europe. Manta ray, sharks, sea horses, moonfish, moray eels and octopus: specimens from the entire range of Mediterranean basin sea-life.

★ **La Barceloneta** (**A** E3)
→ *Between Passeig Joan de Borbó and Passeig Marítim*
The build-up of sedimentation against the harbor dyke (1640) gradually gave rise to a triangular-shaped piece of land which was a magnet for the city's homeless. In 1749, due to progressive urban planning, it was torn down and replaced with a grid pattern of tiny houses for 10,000 fishermen and dockers. A friendly and cheap district with good fish restaurants.

PLAÇA SANT JOSEP ORIOL

CATEDRAL

MUSEU D'HISTÒRIA DE LA CIU

★ Antic Hospital de la Santa Creu (**B** B3)
→ *Carrer de l'Hospital, 56*
Tel. 93 442 71 71
Chapel: Tue-Sat noon–2pm, 4–8pm; Sun 11am–2pm
The eclectic talent of young Barcelonese artists has been given a home in the Gothic chapel of this former hospital (1401). Magnificent patio.

★ Museu d'Art Contemporani de Barcelona / MACBA (**B** B2)
→ *Plaça dels Àngels, 1*
Tel. 93 412 08 10
Mon, Wed-Fri 11am–7.30pm; Sat 10am–8pm; Sun and public hols 10am–3pm
In the heart of El Raval, in an ever-changing working-class area, stands a striking, immaculate building designed by Richard Meier in 1995. The contemporary art museum, or MACBA, contains exhibitions of the latest trends in Catalan and contemporary international art.

★ Centre de Cultura Contemporània de Barcelona (**B** B2)
→ *Carrer de Montalegre, 5*
Tel. 93 306 41 00
Tue-Sat 11am–8pm (10pm Thu)
The remarkable restoration work undertaken here has turned a former orphanage into a modern space. This center (known as the CCCB) juggles different artistic disciplines and mounts a variety of exhibitions and activities. As the headquarters of the internationally renowned Sonar festival, the CCCB more or less institutionalized electronic music.

★ Monestir de Sant Pau del Camp (**B** A4)
→ *Carrer de Sant Pau, 101*
Tel. 93 441 00 01; Cloister: Tue 11.30am–12.30pm; Wed-Mon 11.30am–1pm, 6–7.30pm; Mass: Sat 8pm; Sun noon
In the 10th century, when the original church was built, El Raval was a remote area; today it is one of the city's most densely populated districts. This monastery, with its peaceful little cloister, is the oldest in Barcelona and a rare example of Romanesque architectur

★ La Boqueria (**B** B3) (**Mercat de Sant Josep**
→ *La Rambla, 91*
Mon-Sat 8am–8.30pm
A profusion of stunning, colorful stalls selling spices, fruit, fish and shellfish, cold meats etc. Stop for a glass of freshly squeezed juice, a fruit salad or a *pà amb tomaqu* (bread rubbed with fresh tomato and oil) at one of the bars. The beautiful main hall dates back to 1840, but the market itse would have been here as far back as the 13th cent (outside the city walls). A

↑ Map D

MUSEU D'ART CONTEMPORANI

CENTRE DE CULTURA CONTEMPORÀNIA

ANTIC HOSPITAL DE LA SANTA

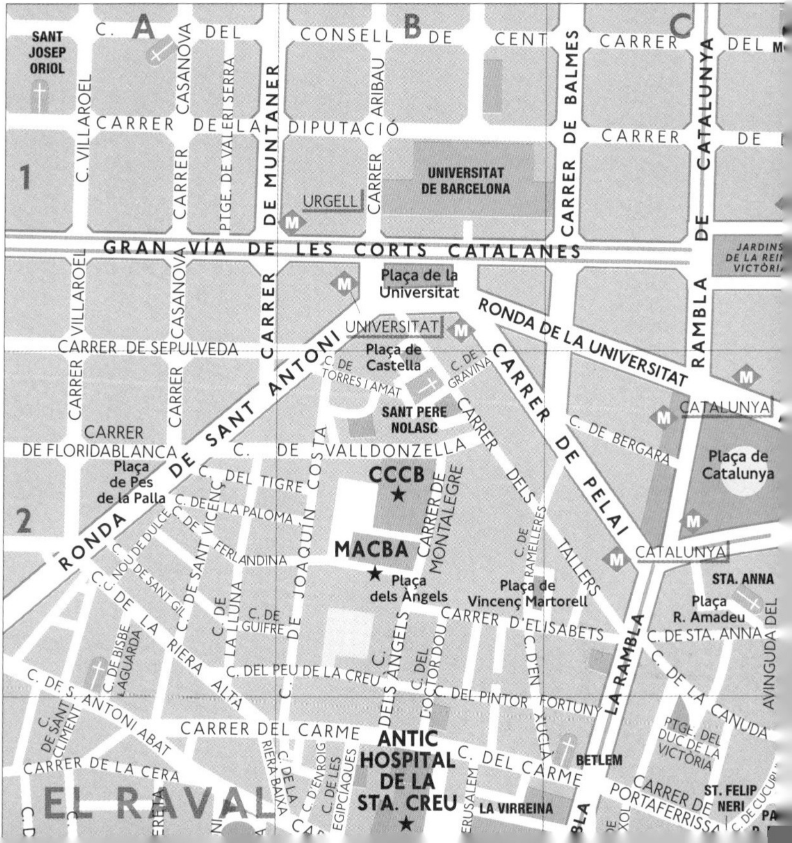

A
B
C
1
2
SANT JOSEP ORIOL
C. DEL CONSELL DE CENT
CARRER DEL M
C. VILLAROEL
CARRER CASANOVA
PTGE. DE VALERI SERRA
CARRER DE MUNTANER
CARRER ARIBAU
CARRER DE BALMES
RAMBLA DE CATALUNYA
CARRER DE LA DIPUTACIÓ
CARRER DE
URGELL
UNIVERSITAT DE BARCELONA
GRAN VÍA DE LES CORTS CATALANES
JARDINS DE LA REI VICTÒRI
Plaça de la Universitat
UNIVERSITAT
RONDA DE LA UNIVERSITAT
CARRER VILLAROEL
CARRER CASANOVA
CARRER
CARRER DE SEPULVEDA
RONDA DE SANT ANTONI
Plaça de Castella
C. DE TORRES I AMAT
C. DE GRAVINA
SANT PERE NOLASC
CARRER DE PELAI
CATALUNYA
C. DE BERGARA
CARRER DE FLORIDABLANCA
C. DE VALLDONZELLA
Plaça de Catalunya
Plaça de Pes de la Palla
C. DEL TIGRE
CCCB
C. DE LA PALOMA
CARRER DELS TALLERS
C. NOU DE DULCE
C. DE SANT VICENÇ
C. DE FERLANDINA
C. DE JOAQUÍN COSTA
MACBA
CARRER DE MONTALEGRE
C. DE RAMELLERES
CATALUNYA
C. DE SANT GIL
C. DE LA LLUNA
Plaça dels Àngels
Plaça de Vincenç Martorell
STA. ANNA
Plaça R. Amadeu
C. DE LA RIERA ALTA
C. DE GUIFRE
CARRER D'ELISABETS
C. DE STA. ANNA
C. DE BISBE LAGUARDA
C. DEL PEU DE LA CREU
C. DELS ÀNGELS
C. DEL DOCTOR DOU
C. D'EN XUCLÀ
LA RAMBLA
AVINGUDA DEL
C. DE LA CANUDA
C. DE S. ANTONI ABAT
C. DEL PINTOR FORTUNY
C. DE SANT CLIMENT
CARRER DEL CARME
PTGE. DEL DUC DE LA VICTÒRIA
C. RIERA BAIXA
C. DE LA
C. D'EN ROIG
C. DE LES EGIPCÍAQUES
ANTIC HOSPITAL DE LA STA. CREU
C. DEL CARME
BETLEM
CARRER DE LA CERA
CARRER DE PORTAFERRISSA
ST. FELIP NERI
C. DE CUCURU
EL RAVAL
JERUSALEM
LA VIRREINA

Representing the city in miniature, these three districts overflow with the elements that make up the true magic of Barcelona: the narrow, disreputable streets of El Raval; the Catalan Gothic architectural gems around the cathedral; and the restored mansions in the old bourgeois district of La Ribera. During the day traditional stores and covered markets draw crowds of tourists and locals alike, with their friendly atmosphere and colorful hustle and bustle. At night the historic heart of the city comes alive, with its numerous tiny bars, trendy clubs and cheap restaurants providing the entertainment.

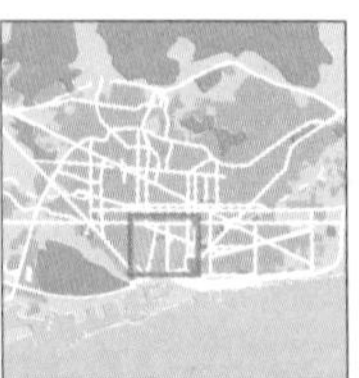

ORGANIC

CASA LEOPOLDO

RESTAURANTS

Romesco (**B** B3)
→ *Carrer de Sant Pau, 28*
Mon-Sat 1pm–midnight
A tiny, noisy room and family cooking at very competitive prices. Don't miss the *frijoles* (kidney beans). Carte €10.

Organic (**B** B3)
→ *Carrer de la Junta de Comerç, 11; Tel. 93 301 09 02*
Daily noon–midnight
An unusual place in a quiet street in the Raval district: colorful, good-quality vegetarian dishes for those who are rather tired of *embotits*. Buffet-style. Set lunch €10.

Casa Alfonso (**B** D2)
→ *Roger de Llúria, 6*
Tel. 93 301 97 83; Mon-Fri 9am–10pm (1am Wed-Fri)
An old traditional *xarcuteria*. Sit at the counter for good tapas in great surroundings. Reasonable prices but uneven service. Carte €20.

Silenus (**B** B2)
→ *Carrer Àngels, 8*
Tel. 93 302 26 80
Mon-Sat 1–5pm, 9pm–midnight (1am Fri-Sat)
It has a quiet atmosphere and a rather minimalist decor with high ceilings and walls dotted with works by local artists. The imaginative, Mediterranean-inspired cuisine changes daily as the chef sees fit. Carte €20.

Espai Sucre (**B** E4)
→ *Carrer de la Princesa, 53*
Tel. 93 268 16 30; Tue-Thu 9–11.30pm; Fri-Sat seatings at 8.30pm and 11pm
This very unusual place only offers desserts – although some of the courses include savory ingredients: cold soup with green apple and spicy yoghurt ice cream, bread pudding with bacon ice cream and pineapple, duck magret with cacao cake and lemon. The dishes are beautifully presented and for each of them a wine is recommended. Quite an experience. Menus €30–50, without wine.

Casa Leopoldo (**B** B3)
→ *Carrer de Sant Rafael, 24*
Tel. 93 441 30 14; Tue-Thu 1.30–4pm, 9 (8.30 Fri-Sat)–11pm; Sun 1.30–4pm
This renowned restaurant, run by the Gil family since 1929, and located in a part of the Raval once famous for its prostitutes, is the haunt of Pepe Carvalho, hero of the detective novels by Vázquez Montalbán, and a lover of good food. Specialties: fish of the day, cooked *a la planxa*; tripe; fried squid. Set menu €45.

CUSTO BARCELONA

EL INGENIO

CAFÉS, TAPAS

Granja M. Viader (**B** B3)
→ *Carrer Xuclà, 4–6*
Tel. 93 318 34 86
Mon 5–8.30pm, Tue-Fri 9am–1.45pm, 5–8.30pm
Whipped cream, rich hot chocolate and biscuits, *mel i mató* (honey and cottage cheese)... Stop at this dairy for breakfast or a quiet afternoon tea away from the buzz of the Rambles.

Bar Pinotxo (**B** B3)
→ *Mercat de la Boqueria, 66–67; Tel. 93 317 17 31*
Mon-Sat 6am–4pm
The most animated kiosk in the market, with a band of followers who keep coming back for the *llagostins* (baby crawfish) *a la planxa* and *guatlles* (quail). Eat at the counter, amid a whirpool of colors, sounds, and smells.

Caelum (**B** C3)
→ *Carrer de la Palla, 8*
Tel. 93 302 69 93; Mon 5–8.30pm; Tue-Sat 10.30am–8.30pm, (midnight Fri-Sat); Sun 11.30am–9pm;
Specialties produced in the monasteries and convents of Spain: *yemas* (made with egg yolk, sugar and almond), *turrón de la abuela* (nougat in dark chocolate) and much more in the basement of these former Jewish baths (14th century).

Cafè Schilling (**B** C4)
→ *Carrer de Ferràn, 23*
Tel. 93 317 67 87
Mon-Sat 10am–2.30am; Sun noon–3am
Of Barcelona's many fashionable cafés, Schilling was the first. Usually packed full, with a cozy atmosphere and old-fashioned decor, this is still a fantastic place for a drink and *entrepans*.

BARS, CLUBS

Boadas Cocktail Bar (**B** C2)
→ *Carrer dels Tallers, 1*
Tel. 93 318 88 26; Mon-Sat noon–2am (3am Fri-Sat)
A small, intimate bar, open since 1933 and very close to La Rambla. Celebrated for its original cocktails, with top marks for the mojitos.

Gurú (**B** B4)
→ *Carrer Nou de la Rambla, 22; Tel. 93 318 08 40*
Daily 5.30pm–3am (bar); 8pm–midnight (restaurant)
At midnight the volume goes up and the tables are pushed away to make room for the dance floor, where an eclectic crowd moves to the sounds of techno until the early hours.

London Bar (**B** B4)
→ *Carrer Nou de la Rambla, 34; Tel. 93 318 52 61*
Tue-Sun 10am–2am (3am Fri-Sat)
Without question, this bar is in a category of its own: all ages, all trends, all types of music. Concerts and shows every evening.

El Copetín (**B** E4)
→ *Passeig del Born, 19*
Tel. 93 319 10 82
Daily 6pm–3am
Set in an area that bursts into life like few others on Saturday nights, this tropical bar pulsates to irresistible Cuban rhythms that make it difficult to remain seated. Excellent cocktails (caïpirinhas, mojitos) provide a further attraction – not to mention the envelopes on offer for customers who want to send personal messages to each other.

SHOPPING

Escriba (**B** C3)
→ *La Rambla, 83; Tel. 93 301 60 27; Daily 9am–9pm*
A famous patisserie with a wonderful Modernist façade, selling delicious chocolates and cookies.

El Manantial de Salud (**B** B3)
→ *Carrer d'en Xuclà, 23*
Tel. 93 301 14 44; Mon-Fri 9am–2pm, 4–8pm (and Sat 9am–2pm, 5–8pm Oct-June)
The most authentic herbalist in Barcelona. Its old cupboards are packed with plants from all over the world. In-store preparation of perfumed oils and all kinds of healing potions.

Custo Barcelona (**B** C4)
→ *Carrer de Ferràn, 36*
Tel. 93 342 66 98
Mon-Sat 10am–10pm; Sun noon–8pm
The celebrated range of clothes of the brothers Dalmau, Custo and David, who became famous in the 1980s for the then daring, colorful T-shirts and accessories inspired by a motorcycle world tour. The exuberant range of men's shirts, women's dresses, blouses, denim, and handbags is now on sale throughout the world.

El Ingenio (**B** C3)
→ *Carrer Rauric, 6*
Tel. 93 317 71 38; Mon-Fri 10am–1.30pm, 4.45–8pm; Sat 11am–2pm, 5–8pm
For masks, balloons and assorted tricks.

El Mercadillo (**B** C3)
→ *Carrer de Portaferrissa, 17*
Daily 11am–9pm
A shopping gallery mostly geared to clubwear. Faded jeans, suede boots, shades and more.

↑ Map D

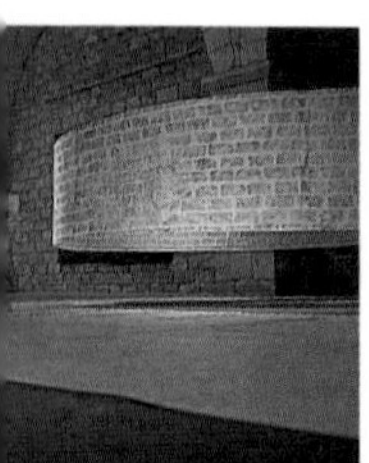

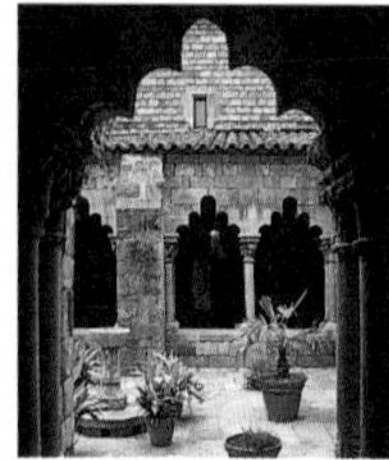

MONESTIR DE ST. PAU DEL CAMP

3x1

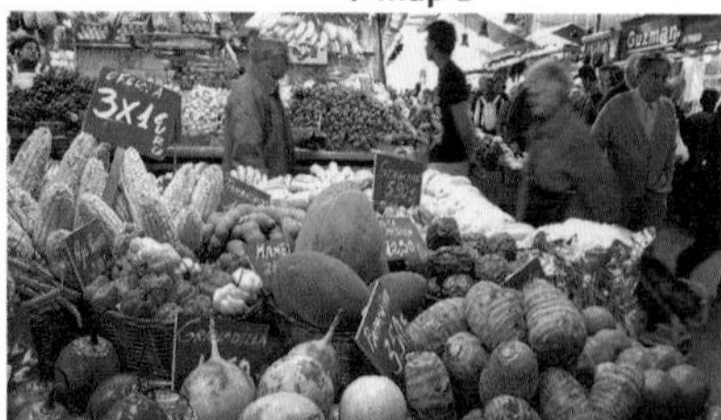

LA BOQUERIA (MERCAT DE SANT JOSEP)

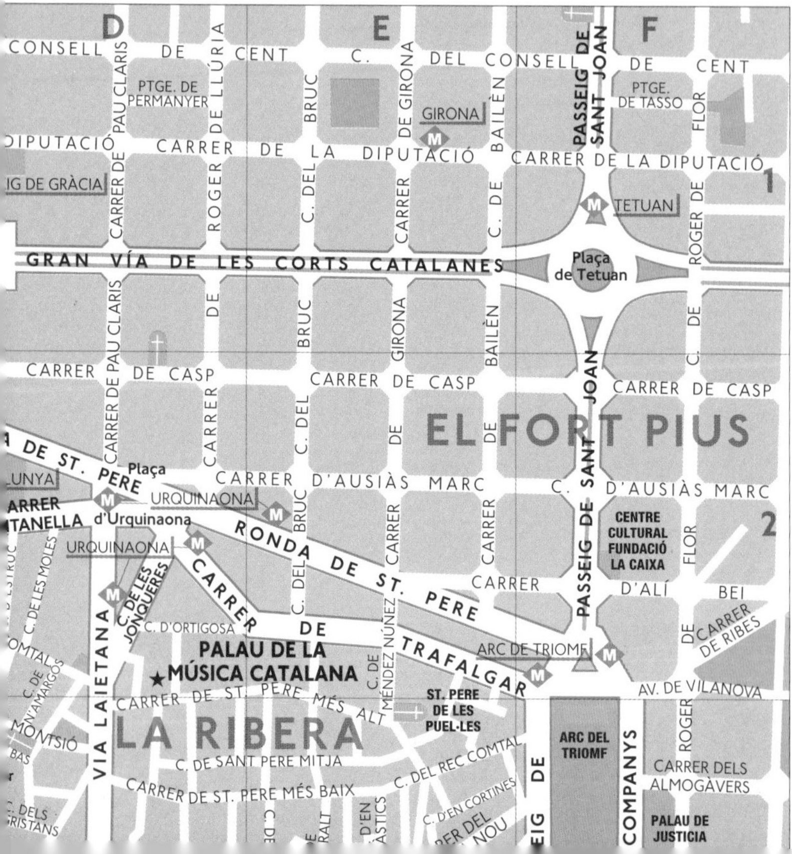

D
E
F
1
2
CONSELL DE CENT
C. DEL CONSELL DE CENT
PTGE. DE PERMANYER
PTGE. DE TASSO
CARRER DE PAU CLARIS
ROGER DE LLÚRIA
C. DEL BRUC
CARRER DE GIRONA
GIRONA
C. DE BAILÈN
PASSEIG DE SANT JOAN
FLOR
DIPUTACIÓ
CARRER DE LA DIPUTACIÓ
CARRER DE LA DIPUTACIÓ
IG DE GRÀCIA
TETUAN
ROGER DE
GRAN VÍA DE LES CORTS CATALANES
Plaça de Tetuan
CARRER DE CASP
CARRER DE CASP
CARRER DE CASP
EL FORT PIUS
A DE ST. PERE
Plaça d'Urquinaona
LUNYA
ARRER
TANELLA
URQUINAONA
URQUINAONA
CARRER D'AUSIÀS MARC
C. D'AUSIÀS MARC
CENTRE CULTURAL FUNDACIÓ LA CAIXA
RONDA DE ST. PERE
CARRER DE TRAFALGAR
CARRER D'ALÍ BEI
CARRER DE RIBES
C. DE LES MOLES
C. DE LES JONQUERES
C. D'ORTIGOSA
PALAU DE LA MÚSICA CATALANA
C. DE MÉNDEZ NÚÑEZ
ARC DE TRIOMF
AV. DE VILANOVA
COMTAL
C. DE N'AMARGÓS
VIA LAIETANA
CARRER DE ST. PERE MÉS ALT
ST. PERE DE LES PUEL·LES
LA RIBERA
MONTSIÓ
ARC DEL TRIOMF
C. DE SANT PERE MITJA
C. DEL REC COMTAL
CARRER DE ST. PERE MÉS BAIX
PASSEIG DE
COMPANYS
ROGER
CARRER DELS ALMOGÀVERS
PALAU DE JUSTICIA
C. DELS GRISTANS
C. D'EN CORTINES
NOU

→ Map F

AÇA ST JAUME

PALAU DE LA MÚSICA CATALANA

onderful feast for the nses.

Santa Maria del Pi / aça Sant Josep Oriol C3)
Between Plaça del Pi and aça Sant Josep Oriol
ily 9.30am–1pm, 5–8.30pm
s the scale of its central ve, one of the largest be found in any Catalan urch, that makes the th-century Gothic basilica Santa Maria del Pi quite ceptional. There are two vely surrounding squares, here an art market is held the first weekend of ch month.

Catedral (**B** D3)
Plaça de la Seu,3
ily 8am– 12.45pm, 5.15–7.30pm; cloister: daily 8.30am–12.30pm, 5.15–7pm
Although most of the cathedral was built from 1298 to 1450, it was not completed until the early 20th century. The building exudes an atmosphere of great harmony and style: the nave, edged with chapels; the choir, with its finely decorated carved stalls; and the cloisters are all good examples of pure Catalan-Gothic. Santa Lucia chapel is the only reminder of the original Romanesque church (9th century). Visit a Sunday morning when the *sardana*, a Catalan dance, takes place in front of the cathedral.

★ Museu d'Història de la Ciutat (**B** D3)
→ Plaça del Rei
Tel. 93 256 21 22; Mon-Thu 10am–2pm, 4–7pm (10am–6pm summer); Fri 10am–2pm
A superb tribute to the history of Barcelona, with drawings and models that describe the development of the city. Underground, spread over 4,784 sq. yds, are the remains of the Roman city of Barcino.

★ Plaça St Jaume (**B** C3)
Plaça St Jaume, remodelled in the 19th century, is the political center of the city, with the two main seats of power facing each other: the Ajuntament (city hall) and the Palau de la Generalitat (regional government). The Baroque salons of the city hall, open on Sunday mornings, are well worth seeing.

★ Palau de la Música Catalana (**B** D2)
→ Carrer Sant Pere més Alt, 11
Tel. 90 244 28 82; Daily 10am–3.30pm (6pm in Aug)
Spectacular Modernist building designed by Domènech i Montaner in 1908. The entrance hall, with its multicolored mosaic-covered pillars, hints at the richness of the interior, whose stained-glass windows and inverted polychrome glass dome bathe the concert hall in a soft light.

PALAU DE PEDRALBES

COL.LEGI DE LES TERESIANES

← Map E

★ **Monestir de Pedralbes** (**C** B1)
→ *Baixada del Monestir, 9*
Tel. 93 203 92 82; Tue-Sun 10am–2pm (5pm April-Sep)
A haven of serenity. This pretty Catalan Gothic-style convent, founded in 1326 and built on three levels around a peaceful garden, still houses members of the Poor Clares. The kitchens, infirmary and cells reveal the nuns' daily life. Part of the Thyssen-Bornemisza collection (the bulk of which is in Madrid) has, since 1993, occupied the former sleeping quarters (works by Fra Angelico, Titian, Rubens and Velázquez).

★ **Finca Güell** (**C** A2)
→ *Avinguda de Pedralbes, 7*
Mon-Fri 9am–noon
A ferocious dragon guards the estate which Eusebi Güell entrusted to Gaudí for restoration in 1884. Drawing on the fashionable neo-Mudejar style, Gaudí redesigned the lodge, the stables and the gate linking the two buildings. Splendid crafted ironwork.

★ **Gardens of the Vil.la Cecília / Parc de la Vil.la Amèlia** (**C** B2)
→ *Carrer de Santa Amèlia*
Daily 10am–6pm (7pm March and Oct; 8pm April and Sep; 9pm May-Aug)
Two gardens set on either side of a small, ordinary-looking street. That of the Vil.la Cecília is a maze of tall hedges and contains a curious bronze sculpture of a drowning woman. Opposite is the more traditional Vil.la Amèlia park, with a pond in the center and benches scattered here and there.

★ **Palau de Pedralbes** (**C** A2)
→ *Avinguda Diagonal, 686*
Tel. 93 280 13 64
Museums: Tue-Sun 10am–6pm (3pm Sun). Garden: daily 10am–8pm
Two interesting museums housed in a former palace (1919) which was inspired by Italian Renaissance mansions. One, the Museum of Decorative Arts, exhibits Catalan, medieval-style decoratio and furniture. In the othe the Ceramics Museum, is an exceptional collecti of Spanish ceramics and medieval pottery. Splend fountain-bench in the pa designed by Gaudí.

★ **Col.legi de les Teresianes** (**C** D2)
→ *Carrer de Ganduxer, 85–105; Tel. 93 212 33 54; Visit in groups and by appt, Sat 11am–1pm; closed July-Aug*
Behind the severe brick façade of this religious establishment lies a rich

MONESTIR DE PEDRALBES

JARDINS DE LA VIL.LA CECÍLIA

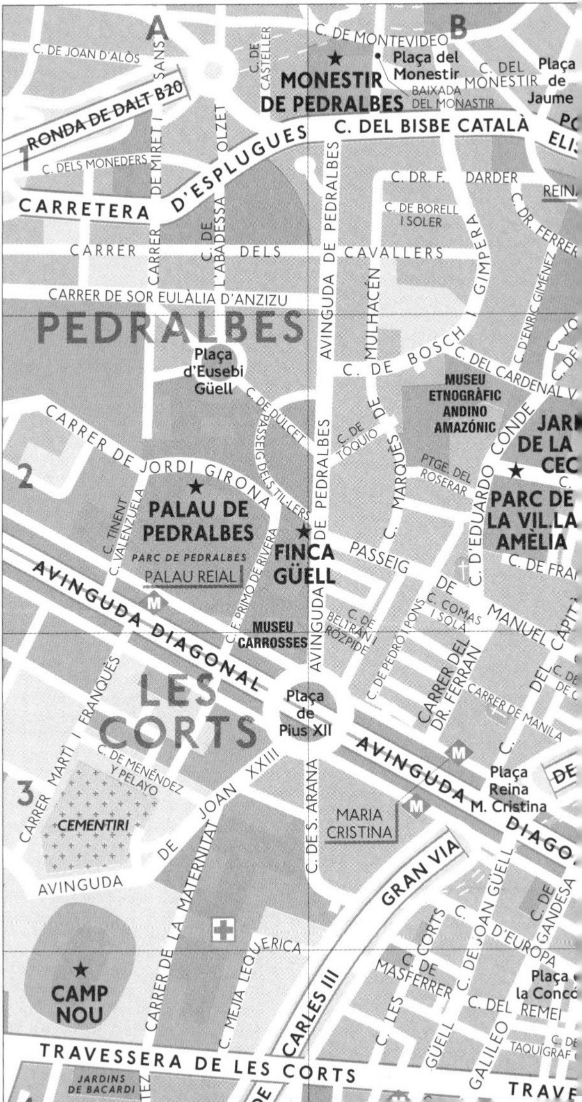

A
B
1
2
3
C. DE JOAN D'ALÒS
SANS
C. DE CASTELLER
C. DE MONTEVIDEO
Plaça del Monestir
C. DEL MONESTIR
Plaça de Jaume
MONESTIR DE PEDRALBES
BAIXADA DEL MONASTIR
RONDA DE DALT B20
C. DE MIRET I SANS
OLZET
C. DEL BISBE CATALÀ
C. DELS MONEDERS
CARRETERA D'ESPLUGUES
C. DR. F. DARDER
C. DE BORELL I SOLER
C. DR. FERRER
C. DE L'ABADESSA OLZET
CARRER DELS CAVALLERS
CARRER DE SOR EULÀLIA D'ANZIZU
PEDRALBES
AVINGUDA DE PEDRALBES
MULHACÉN
C. DE BOSCH I GIMPERA
C. D'ENRIC GIMÉNEZ
Plaça d'Eusebi Güell
C. DEL CARDENAL V
MUSEU ETNOGRÀFIC ANDINO AMAZÓNIC
C. DE DULCET
PASSEIG DELS TIL·LERS
C. DE TÒQUIO
C. DE MARQUÈS
CARRER DE JORDI GIRONA
JARDINS DE LA CEC
PTGE. DEL ROSERAR
C. D'EDUARDO CONDE
PALAU DE PEDRALBES
PARC DE PEDRALBES
PALAU REIAL
C. TINENT C. VALENZUELA
FINCA GÜELL
PARC DE LA VIL.LA AMÈLIA
C. DE FRA
PASSEIG DE MANUEL GIRONA
C. E. PRIMO DE RIVERA
AVINGUDA DIAGONAL
M
MUSEU CARROSSES
C. DE BELTRAN I RÓZPIDE
C. COMAS I SOLÀ
C. DE PEDRÓ I PONS
CARRER DEL DR. FERRAN
CARRER DE MANILA
LES CORTS
Plaça de Pius XII
CARRER MARTÍ I FRANQUÈS
C. DE MENÉNDEZ Y PELAYO
AVINGUDA DE JOAN XXIII
C. DE S. ARANA
Plaça Reina M. Cristina
MARIA CRISTINA
CEMENTIRI
CARRER DE LA MATERNITAT
GRAN VIA
C. DE JOAN GÜELL
C. DE GANDESA
C. MEJIA LEQUERICA
C. D'EUROPA
C. DE MASFERRER
C. LES CORTS
CAMP NOU
CARLES III
Plaça de la Concó
C. DEL REMEI
GALILEO
C. DE TAQUIGRAF
TRAVESSERA DE LES CORTS
JARDINS DE BACARDI

Situated around the imposing, seemingly endless Avinguda Diagonal, the busy, commercial thoroughfare running northwest to southeast across Barcelona, the villages of Sarrià, Pedralbes and Sants are now mainly residential areas. In Sarrià, the atmosphere is largely that of an exclusive provincial town (the best schools are here), especially in the residential back streets away from the main drag. The monumental Pedralbes ('the white stones'), complete with palace and gardens, is on the west side and runs to the city limits. Sants is more sparsely populated and features a modern railway station.

EL VELL SARRIÀ

A CONTRALUZ

RESTAURANTS

Bene Asai (**C** D2)
→ *Carrer del Doctor Carulla, 61; Tel. 93 434 06 77*
Mon-Sat 1.30–4pm, 8.30–11.30pm; Sun 1.30–4pm
A tiny restaurant especially popular with the younger, local crowd. Good pasta and pizza are served in the plain dining room at the back, or outside on the small terrace in summer. Carte €20.

La Botiga (**C** D4)
→ *Avinguda de Josep Tarradellas, 155 (three other branches); Tel. 93 410 27 04; Mon-Fri 8am–4.30pm, 8pm–midnight; Sat-Sun 1pm–1am*
Creative Catalan dishes prepared with ingredients that are brought straight from the market – and illustrated in the paintings on the walls. Healthy and reliable. Carte €20–25.

La Vaquería (**C** C4)
→ *Carrer de Deu i Mata, 141*
Tel. 93 419 07 35
Mon-Fri 1.30–4pm, 9pm–12.30am; Sat 9pm–12.30am
Three different areas with three distinct moods, in a tastefully refurbished cowshed: piano-bar, disco and unpretentious restaurant, whose gamble to offer imaginative, tasty fare at a good price has certainly paid off. Set menus: €19 (lunch), € 35 (dinner).

Negro (**C** C3)
→ *Avinguda Diagonal, 640*
Tel. 93 405 94 44
Daily 1.30–4pm, 8.30pm–midnight (1am Thu-Sat)
The designer decor obviously tries to conjure up images of New York. The cooking is in a class of its own, combining Mediterranean ingredients with Oriental know-how: Japanese-style chicken kebabs, tuna fish tartare, cured spiced beef, Thai curry rice. Lunch menu €17. Carte €30–35.

El Vell Sarrià (**C** C1)
→ *Carrer Major de Sarrià 93*
Tel. 93 204 57 10
Tue-Sat 1.30–3.30pm, 9–11.30pm; Sun 1.30–3.30pm
Sarrià has retained its provincial atmosphere, and this restaurant, in a house typical of the area, is probably the best establishment of its kind in the district, situated in a back alley away from the more touristy streets. On the menu, Catalan, rice-based specialties with seasonal variations: mountain rice with mushrooms (with rabbit and *botifarra* – a black sausage cooked in white

R TOMÁS

FOIX DE SARRIÀ

PEDRALBES CENTRE

wine); rice with artichoke, crab, shrimp and mushrooms; wild boar in redcurrant sauce, and more. Carte €35–40.

A Contraluz (**C** D2)
→ *Carrer Milanesat, 19*
Tel. 93 203 06 58
Daily 1.30–4pm, 8.30pm–midnight (1am Fri-Sat)
Still one of the most fashionable terraces in town, complete with trailing jasmine and candles. Seasonal cuisine, modern Mediterranean in style. Vegetables, risottos and desserts – all utterly delicious. Carte €35–40.

CAFÉS, TAPAS

Tejada (**C** D4)
→ *Carrer del Tenor Viñas, 3*
Tel. 93 200 73 41; Daily 10am–1.30am (2am Fri-Sat)
With a garden close by, this bar is an essential stop-off for its huge tapas menu and the bustle that seems to prevail here, day and night.

Bar Tomàs (**C** C2)
→ *Carrer Major de Sarrià, 49; Tel. 93 203 10 77*
Mon-Tue, Thu-Sun noon–4pm, 6–10pm
Everyone in Barcelona agrees: the best *patatas bravas* (fried potato in a spicy sauce) to be found in the city are those on the menu at Bar Tomàs. Crisp and crunchy on the outside, soft on the inside and served with perfect sauces. The bar is always packed. *Patatas bravas* and beer €3.20.

CLUBS, DISCOS

Zacarías (**C** D4)
→ *Avinguda Diagonal, 477*
Tel. 93 319 17 89
Daily 11pm–5.30am
Techno music; live pop, rock, jam-session early evenings.

Elephant (**C** A2)
→ *Passeig dels Til·lers, 1*
Tel. 93 203 75 46
Thu-Sat 11.30pm–4.30am
This fashionable club, set in an old house, attracts some of the city's more elegant night birds. The splendid garden provides an added attraction in fine weather.

Bikini (**C** C4)
→ *Carrer de Deu i Mata, 105*
Tel. 93 322 08 00
Wed-Sat 2–5am
A famous club which has now reopened but is sticking to the formula which made it popular in the first place: one room is devoted to 1980s and 1990s music, another offers Latin rhythms to sway to, and a bar for cocktails and snacks.

Up & Down (**C** C3)
→ *Carrer de Numància, 179*
Tel. 93 205 51 94
Tue, Thu-Sat 2–6am
'Up' – a restaurant and private club where the disco music always incorporates the latest sounds. 'Down' – a mixture of rock music and over-the-top *sevillanas*.

SHOPPING

Foix de Sarrià (**C** C1)
→ *Carrer Major de Sarrià, 57*
Tel. 93 203 07 14
Daily 8am–9pm
A hundred-year-old establishment offering specialties that never go out of fashion, like *petxines* – shell-shaped, chocolate-covered almond cookies. Try the delicious homemade *horchata* (a drink made from the almond-like *chufa* fruit, originally from Valencia but very popular in Barcelona), the ice creams and the mousses. Everything tastes great.

Lafuente (**C** D3)
→ *Carrer de Johann Sebastian Bach, 20*
Tel. 93 201 15 13
Mon-Fri 9am–2pm, 4.30–8.30pm; Sat 9am–2pm
A bodega spread over 1,076 square feet where you can find 99 percent of the wines available on the Spanish market. Also on sale is a huge variety of liquors from all over the world.

Semon (**C** D3)
→ *Carrer de Ganduxer, 31*
Tel. 93 201 65 08
Mon-Sat 10am–2.30pm, 5–9pm; Sun 10am–2pm
A well-known deli-*xarcuteria*. In one corner is a tiny restaurant where you can try the goodies.

Centros comerciales (**C** B3 to D4)
There is a concentration of shopping centers along one section of the Avinguda Diagonal. It's paradise for shopaholics, especially during the sales.

El Corte Inglés
→ *Avinguda Diagonal, 617*
Tel. 93 366 71 00
Daily 10am–10pm
The most Spanish of the department stores. A must.

Pedralbes Centre
→ *Avinguda Diagonal, 609*
Tel. 93 410 68 21
Mon-Sat 10.30am–9pm
Chic, designer shopping.

L'Illa Diagonal
→ *Avinguda Diagonal, 545*
Tel. 93 444 00 00
Mon-Sat 10.30am–9pm
Huge and cosmopolitan.

C D

1 2 3

Plaça d'Amich
C. DE RAMON MIQUEL I PLANAS
LA REINA DE MONTCADA
CARRER L'AVIÓ PLUS ULTRA
VIA AUGUSTA
CARRER D'ANGLÍ
DE MARGENAT
C. DE DOLORS MONSERDÀ
C. DE POMARET
CARRER D'IRADIER
C. DELS PLANELLA
C. DE LES ESCOLES PIES
C. DE LA MARQUESA DE VILALLONGA
C. DE L'ESPERANÇA
C. DE NEGREVERNIS
Plaça de Sarrià
C. DE SETANTÍ
C. DE SARRIÀ
PASSEIG DE LA BONANOVA
CARRER DE CALATRAVA
C. ROUX
CARRER DE DALMASES
C. DEL PEDRÓ DE LA CREU
C. DE JAUME PIQUET
C. MAJOR
CARRER DEL CARDENAL SENTMENAT
SARRIÀ
JARDINS DOCTOR ROIG RAVENTOS
CARRER DE L'EMANCIPACIÓ
C. DE BONAPLATA
Plaça de St. Vicenç de Sarrià
SARRIA
C. PAU ALCOVER
C. DEL DOCTOR CARULLA
CARRER DE FONTCOBERTA
CARRER DELS VERGÓS
Plaça de l'Orient
C. DE GANDUXER
Plaça d'Artós
C. DE R. BATLLE
Plaça de Joaquim Pena
C. DE VERGÓS
C. DE CARRENCÀ
C. D'ALACANT
Plaça de F. Casablancas
C. DEL MILANESAT
LES TRES TORRES
C. DEL DOCTOR ROUX
COL.LEGI DE LES TERESIANES
C. BENET MATEU
PG. DE ST. JOAN BOSCO
C. DE ROSARI
VIA AUGUSTA
GENERAL MITRE
C. DE MARIA AUXILIADORA
C. DE CASTELLNOU
C. DE LA NENA CASAS
C. DE VICO
CARRER ALT DE GIRONELLA
Plaça de Gironella
LA BONANOVA
FINCA MIRALLES
C. DE MODOLELL
Plaça de Prat de la Riba
C. DE BUIGAS
Plaça d'Eguilaz
C. DE LES TRES TORRES
C. DE LES ESCOLES PIES
RONDA DEL
C. DEL LÀZARO CÀRDENAS
C. DE LA REINA VICTÒRIA
C. DE VALLMAJOR
NUMÀNCIA
AVINGUDA DE SARRIÀ
C. DE LA CARAVEL·LA LA NIÑA
C. DE CAN RABIA
C. DEL DR. FLEMING
C. DE J. BENAVENTE
CARRER DE GANDUXER
Plaça de Sant Gregori Taumaturg
TEMPLE
C. DE J. S. BACH
C. DE JOSEP BERTRAND
C. DE BORI I FONTESTÀ
CARRER DE CALVET
JARDINS DEL POETA E. MARQUINA
C. DEL TENOR VIÑAS
AVINGUDA DE SARRIÀ
CARRER DE
JARDINS DE SANT JOAN DE DÉU
Plaça del Prat
CARRER DE DEU I MATA
C. DEL TAQUÍGRAF
TENÇA
Plaça de J. Llongueras
C. DEL MESTRE NICOLAU
AV. DE PAU CASALS
DIAGONAL

FINCA MIRALLES/ STATUE DE GAUDÍ

CAMP NOU

↑ Map D

PARC DE L'ESPANYA INDUSTRIAL

PARC JOAN MIRÓ

Map E →

erior: shafts of light, tios and parabolic-hed corridors. Putting de the economic and listic constraints posed by the order of int Theresa in his nstruction of this 1889 ilding, Gaudí proved that was a fine architect of ucture as well as a nius of form.

Finca Miralles (C B2-3)
Passeig de Manuel ona, 55–61
front of an astonishing saic-covered outer wall, signed by Gaudí in 1901, nds a bronze statue ich pays homage the master himself.

★ Plaça dels Països Catalans (C B-C5)
Laid out in 1983 by Viaplana and Piñon, architects of the superb CCCB building in El Raval (see **B**), this avant-garde square has been the subject of much controversy. Spartan, open to the elements, and located at a crossover of roads and railway lines, it shows that even simple concrete and metal shelters can be appealing.

★ Camp Nou (C A4)
→ Av. de Joan XXIII, Carrer Arístides Maillol
Tel. 93 496 36 08; Museum: Mon-Sat 10am–8pm; Sun and public hols 10am–3pm
Barcelona's citizens love their football, and they love Barça (FC Barcelona). This ancient rival to the Real Madrid team has become a symbol of the Catalan identity. The stadium, home-ground to the players in *blaugrana* (blue and maroon), and one of the largest in Europe, was built in 1957. A museum traces the history of the club since 1889.

★ Parc de l'Espanya Industrial (C B6)
→ Plaça de Joan Peiró
Daily 10am–6pm (7pm March and Oct; 8pm April and Sep; 9pm May-Aug)
A subtle dialogue between nature, contemporary art and modern architecture, this park, which backs onto the station at Sants, is built on the site of a former textile factory. Unusual view over the sculptures from the top of the ten lighthouses surrounding the lake.

★ Parc Joan Miró (C C6)
→ Carrer de Tarragona
Daily 10am–6pm (7pm March and Oct; 8pm April and Sep; 9pm May-Aug)
The former slaughterhouses have now disappeared and in their place stands this park, created in the 1980s. The highlights here are the palm grove, the playgrounds, a pergola and Miró's *Bird Lady*.

PALAU BARÓ DE QUADRAS

LA PEDRERA

★ Avinguda del Tibidabo (**D** B1)
→ *By tram from Av. del Tibidabo Station to Plaça del Doctor Andreu; Sat-Sun and public hols 10am–6pm (8pm in summer)*
Old trams (*tramvia blau*), in service since 1902, run along this avenue lined with modernist buildings. At the end there are breathtakingly clear views over the city and the bay. Anyone who likes heights should take the funicular up to the fairground.

★ Parc Güell (**D** D2)
→ *Carrer d'Olot; Daily 10am–6pm (7pm March and Oct; 8pm April and Sep; 9pm May-Aug)*
Commissionned by Count Güell to Gaudí, this bizarre and jubilant design was originally planned to be a garden suburb. The business went bust, however, and by 1914 only the entrance to the park and the open-air installations had been completed. Don't miss the vast hall whose ceiling is supported by 86 inclined columns, the staircase with its mosaic salamander and the undulating bench, on which remain some of the original *trencadís* – a type of mosaic created from broken tile shards, which Gaudi and his follower Jujol, were the first to use.

★ Casa Terrades (**D** C5)
→ *Av. Diagonal, 416–420*
The House of Spires (1903), with its six towers, has the air of a northern European castle. This masterpiece, by Puig i Cadafalch, is strongly influenced by neogothic architecture.

★ La Pedrera (**D** B5-6)
→ *Passeig de Gràcia, 92*
Tel. 93 484 55 30
Daily 9.30am–8pm; concerts 10pm–midnight in July
All undulations, hollows and humps, the façade of the Casa Milà, known as La Pedrera (literally 'the quarry'), resembles a cliff eroded by years of sea and wind. Gaudí designed this building at the height of his career in 1905, fashioning the materials and giving form to his extraordinary, overflowing fantasy in everything from the grou floor columns to the surr chimneys on top. Many feats of architecture insic such as the absence of load-bearing walls.

★ Fundació Antoni Tàpies (**D** B6)
→ *Carrer d'Aragó, 255*
Tel. 93 487 03 15
Tue-Sun 10am–8pm
This splendid building, th first example of Modernis architecture (1879), gave Domènech i Montaner ar opportunity to put into practice his principles of rationalist construction, while drawing on a neo-Mudejar style. Today the

← Map B

AVINGUDA DEL TIBIDABO

PARC GÜELL

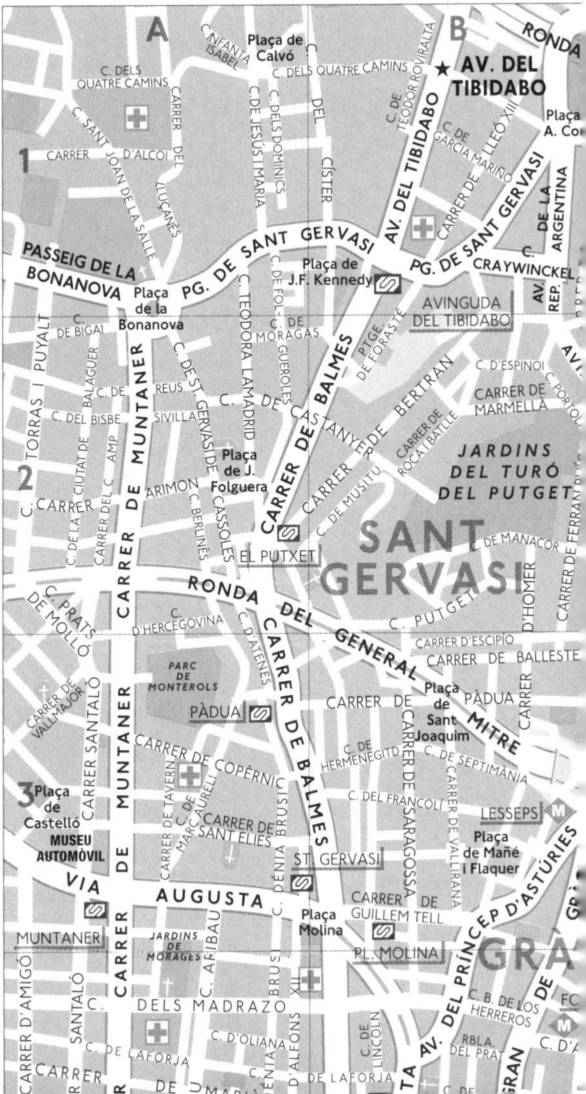

A
B
1
2
3

Plaça de Calvó
C. INFANTA ISABEL
C. DELS QUATRE CAMINS
C. DELS QUATRE CAMINS
C. DE TEODOR ROVIRALTA
★ AV. DEL TIBIDABO
RONDA
Plaça A. Co
C. SANT JOAN DE LA SALLE
CARRER D'ALCOI
CARRER DEL LLUÇANÈS
C. DE JESÚS I MARIA
C. DELS DOMINICS
C. DEL CÍSTER
AV. DEL TIBIDABO
C. DE GARCIA MARIÑO
CARRER DE LLEÓ XIII
PG. DE SANT GERVASI
DE LA ARGENTINA
PASSEIG DE LA BONANOVA
Plaça de la Bonanova
PG. DE SANT GERVASI
Plaça de J.F. Kennedy
PG. DE SANT GERVASI
C. CRAYWINCKEL
AV. REP.
AVINGUDA DEL TIBIDABO
C. DE BIGAI
C. TEODORA LAMADRID
C. DE FOLGUEROLES
C. DE MORAGAS
PTGE. DE FORASTÉ
C. D'ESPINOI
C. TORRAS I PUYALT
C. DE BALAGUER
C. DE REUS
C. DE ST. GERVASI DE CASSOLES
C. DE CASTANYER
CARRER DE BALMES
CARRER DE BERTRAN
CARRER DE MARMELLÀ
C. PORTOLÀ
C. DEL BISBE SIVILLA
CARRER DE ROCA I BATLLE
JARDINS DEL TURÓ DEL PUTGET
CARRER DE MUNTANER
C. DE LA CIUTAT DE BALAGUER
CARRER DEL C. AMP
Plaça de J. Folguera
CARRER ARIMON
C. BERLINÈS
CARRER DE MUSITU
C. DE MUSITU
SANT GERVASI
C. DE MANACOR
CARRER DE FERRAN PUIG
EL PUTXET
RONDA DEL GENERAL MITRE
C. PRATS DE MOLLÓ
C. D'HERCEGOVINA
C. D'ATENES
CARRER DE BALMES
C. PUTGET
D'HOMER
CARRER D'ESCIPIÓ
CARRER DE BALLESTE
PARC DE MONTEROLS
PÀDUA
CARRER DE VALLMAJOR
CARRER SANTALÓ
CARRER DE MUNTANER
CARRER DE PÀDUA
Plaça de Sant Joaquim
CARRER DE SARAGOSSA
C. DE HERMENEGILD
C. DE SEPTIMÀNIA
CARRER DE COPÈRNIC
C. DEL FRANCOLÍ
CARRER DE VALLIRANA
Plaça de Castelló
MUSEU AUTOMÒVIL
CARRER DE TAVERN
C. DE MARC AURELI
CARRER DE SANT ELIES
C. DÉNIA
BRUSI
LESSEPS
Plaça de Mañé i Flaquer
ST. GERVASI
VIA AUGUSTA
CARRER DE GUILLEM TELL
Plaça Molina
AV. DEL PRÍNCEP D'ASTÚRIES
MUNTANER
JARDINS DE MORAGES
C. ARIBAU
PL. MOLINA
GRÀ
CARRER D'AMIGÓ
C. SANTALÓ
C. DELS MADRAZO
C. ALFONS XII
C. DE LINCOLN
C. B. DE LOS HERREROS
GRAN DE
C. DE LAFORJA
C. D'OLIANA
RBLA. DEL PRAT
C. DE LAFORJA
CARRER

After the demolition of the fortified city walls in the 1850s, 'L'Eixample' (literally 'expansion'), was the result of a plan by engineer Ildefons Cerdà to come up with an egalitarian, rational program of town-planning. He built a democratic, grid-like district which links the old city with the suburbs. Because of its many stunning Modernist designs the district has become a favorite area for visitors with an interest in architecture, although it is also known today as Barcelona's main gay area. To the north, the more working-class Gràcia is like a village, with its dense web of streets and squares. Here cafés, bars, and restaurants attract a more youthful and bohemian crowd.

EL JAPONÉS DEL TRAGALUZ

FLASH-FLASH

RESTAURANTS

Flash Flash (**D** B4)
→ *Carrer de la Granada del Penedès, 25; Tel. 93 237 09 90; Daily 1pm–1.30am*
The ultimate in tasty *truites* and Pop art. Opened in the 1970s, this was once the hangout of the 'divine left' (a movement which united intellectuals and architects). Even today it is a great place to be seen. Good hamburgers too, but keep room for dessert and the rum omelet. Carte €18–20.

Madrid-Barcelona (**D** B6)
→ *Carrer d'Aragó, 282 Tel. 93 215 70 27; Daily 1–4pm, 8.30–midnight*
This eatery has built its reputation on simple yet mouthwatering Catalan specialties. Try their famous *xai a les dotze cabeces d'all* (baked lamb with 12 cloves of garlic). Carte €20.

El Japonés del Tragaluz (**D** B5)
→ *Passatge de la Concepció, 2; Tel. 93 487 25 92 Daily 1.30–4pm, 8.30pm–midnight (8pm–1am Fri-Sat)*
A japanese restaurant with designer decor and techno background music. Behind the steel counter, cooks clad in smart black kimonos prepare tempura, sushi, and *kushiyaki* (skewers). Carte €15–20.

Casa Amàlia (**D** C6)
→ *Passatge Mercat, 4–6 Tel. 93 458 94 58; Tue-Sun 1–3.30pm, 9–10.30pm; closed Aug and Sun in July*
Located in a narrow passageway, away from the agitation, it offers a breezy menu of freshly prepared dishes, using the best produce that its neighbor the covered Concepció market has to offer that day. Set lunch €11. Carte €25–30.

Bilbao (**D** C5)
→ *Carrer del Perill, 33 Tel. 93 458 96 24; Mon-Sat 1 (2pm Sat)–4pm, 9–11pm*
A classic restaurant which has relied on serving unfussy, high quality traditional cuisine for the past 50 years. *Bacalao* (cod) specialties. Carte €35–40.

La Balsa (**D** A1)
→ *Carrer Infanta Isabel, 4 Tel. 93 211 50 48 Mon 8.30–11.30pm; Tue-Sat 1.30–3.30pm, 8.30–11.30pm; Sun 1.30–3.30pm*
Set above the city, in the heart of luxuriant greenery, this is a Barcelonese favorite. Imaginative seasonal Catalan cuisine is served in a very pleasant dining room with large bay windows. There is also a

É DEL SOL

LUZ DE GAS

VINÇON

lovely, flower-laden terrace. Carte €55.

Tragaluz (**D** B5)
→ *Passatge de la Concepció, 5; Tel. 93 487 06 21; Daily 1.30–4pm, 8.30pm–midnight*
Traditional Catalan cuisine, lightened by a touch of creativity, for a romantic dinner under a huge beautiful slanted roof of glass and metallic beams. Those with less time to spare will prefer salads, *entrepans* and pasta in the Tragarràpid on the ground floor. Set lunch menu €26; carte €50.

Gaig (**D** B4)
→ *Hotel Cram, Carrer Aragó, 214; Tel. 93 429 1017 Mon 9–11pm; Tue-Sat 1.30–3.30pm, 9–11pm*
Michelin-starred, Catalan haute cuisine by fourth generation chef-owner Carles Gaig. Reservations advised. Carte €32–45.

Moo (**D** B5)
→ *Hotel Omm, Carrer Rosselló 265 Tel. 93 445 4000 Daily 1.30–4pm, 8.30–11pm*
Another superb restaurant with a clean, modern decor, a bamboo-planted garden and small jewel-like sculptures on the tables. Modern gourmet Mediterranean cuisine by chef Felip Llufriu. Reserve in advance. Carte €50.

CAFÉS, BAR, TAPAS

Molina Xarcuteria (**D** B3)
→ *Plaça Molina, 1; Daily 8am–9.45pm (3pm Sun)*
A traditional deli with the best *embotits* and Catalan specialties: *botifarra*, ham, *fuet*. Everything can be eaten in or taken out.

Bar París (**D** A5)
→ *Carrer de París, 187 Daily 7am–2am (3am Fri-Sat)*
This noisy, friendly, long-established bar continues to attract a young crowd. Large-portioned tapas.

Gimlet (**D** A4)
→ *Carrer Santaló, 46 Tel. 93 201 53 06; Daily 7pm–2.30am (3am Fri-Sat)*
Two-thirds gin to one-third lime juice: the favorite cocktail of Philip Marlowe, Raymond Chandler's detective, has given its name to this cozy bar. The tapas at next-door's Casa Fernández are a good bet for anyone in need of sustenance.

Plaça del Sol, Plaça de la Virreina
These squares are Gràcia's main attraction, where the cafés are always full to brimming.

Café del Sol (**D** B4)
→ *Plaça del Sol, 16 Daily 12.30pm–2.30am*
Good tapas; sunny terrace.

Virreina (**D** C4)
→ *Plaça de la Virreina, 1 Daily 10am–1am*
Delicious sandwiches.

NIGHTCLUBS

Otto Zutz (**D** B4)
→ *Carrer de Lincoln, 15 Tel. 93 238 07 22; Tue-Sat 11.30pm–5am (6am Thu-Sat)*
Opened in 1985 this club found immediate success with its post-industrial decor and the talent of its DJs. Each room has its own sound, from funk to uncompromising techno. Admission €10–15.

Universal (**D** A4)
→ *Carrer de Marià Cubí, 184 Tel. 93 201 35 96; Mon-Sat 11pm–3.30am (5am Thu-Sat)*
A hip two-storey club, full of beautiful people. House music downstairs and a cozy salon upstairs.

Luz de Gas (**D** A4)
→ *Carrer de Muntaner, 246 Tel. 93 209 77 11 Daily 11.30pm–5am*
Set in a former red-and-gold music-hall. Jazz and blues concerts every night from midnight.

Sweet Café (**D** A6)
→ *Carrer de Casanova 75 Tue-Sun 8pm–2.30/3am*
This cozy bar and club popular with (but by no means reserved to) the gay community hosts a wide range of events: live DJ sessions, short film festivals, art exhibitions, etc.

SHOPPING

Mauri (**D** B6)
→ *Rambla de Catalunya, 102 Mon-Sat 8am (9am Sat)–9pm; Sun 9am–3pm*
Delicious brioches and pastries. Tearoom upstairs.

Quilez (**D** B6)
→ *Rambla de Catalunya, 63 Mon-Fri 9am–2pm, 4.30–8.30pm; Sat 9am–2pm*
Stunning window display with hundreds of different preserves: anchovies cockles, mussels. Inside, a huge range of beers, wines and liquors.

Vinçon (**D** B6)
→ *Passeig de Gràcia, 96 Tel. 93 215 60 50 Mon-Sat 10am–8.30pm*
A must for anyone interested in design since its opening in 1941, the three-story store is filled with classic pieces and the latest creations, big and small covetable household and office accessories at affordable prices.

Boulevard Rosa (**D** B6)
→ *Passeig de Gràcia, 55 Mon-Sat 10.30am–9pm*
More than 70 elegant shops under one roof, reflecting the city's latest trends in fashion.

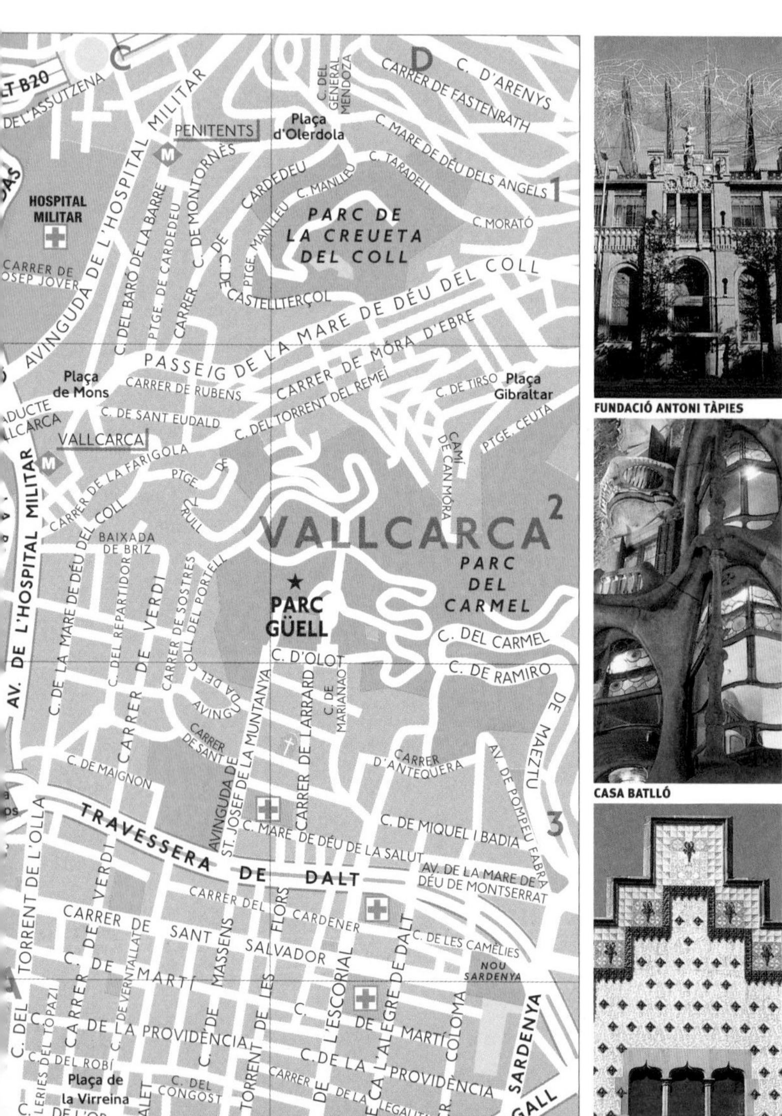

FUNDACIÓ ANTONI TÀPIES

CASA BATLLÓ

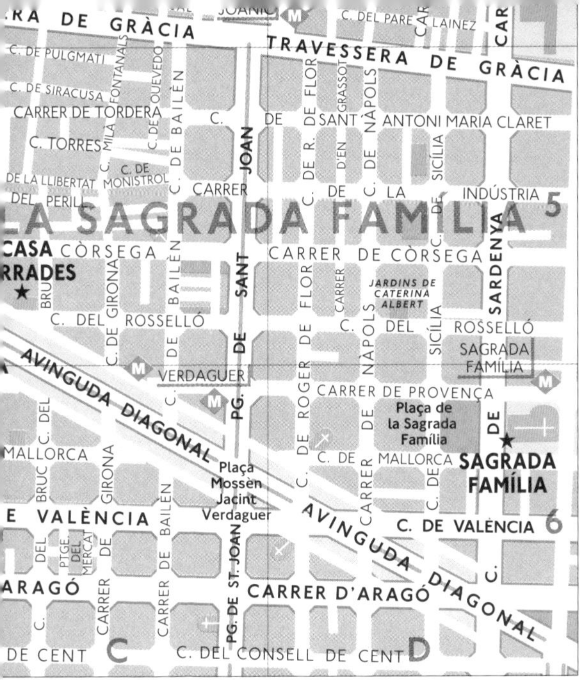

CASA LLEÓ MORERA

SAGRADA FAMÍLIA

Map F →

ılding is topped by
vire sculpture by Tàpies.
e foundation houses the
ıst complete collection
the artist's work.

**Palau Baró
Quadras** (**D** B5)
*Avinguda Diagonal, 373
93 238 73 37; Mon-Fri
ım–8pm; Sun 10am–2pm*
ɪpired by the spatial
ɪout used in Gothic
hitecture, this palau by
'g i Cadafalch (1902) is
ilt around a central patio.
e hall, staircase and
ble floor (admission free)
: of special interest.
e Casa Asia is a cultural
nter devoted to Asia.

Casa Amatller (**D** B6)
*Passeig de Gràcia, 41
Tel. 93 487 72 17; Undergoing restoration but guided tours Mon-Fri mornings by appt; www.amatller.org*
Another example of Puig i Cadafalch's ability to draw on the neogothic style and yet break with the geometric rigor of the Eixample. The façade is that of a medieval palace from a Hanseatic city.

★ **Casa Batlló** (**D** B6)
*→ Passeig de Gràcia, 43
Tel. 93 216 03 06
Daily 9am–8pm*
Fabulously poetic creation by Gaudí (1904) for the industrialist Josep Batlló. The roof resembles a giant saurian's spine while the base of the columns are reminiscent of enormous elephants' feet. Covered in tiny pieces of multicolored glass shards, the twinkling façade appears as if covered in fish scales. The interior is an extension of this dream-like world: light shafts, shimmering stained-glass windows and a swirling false ceiling. The wrought iron work on the balcony and staircase banister is also remarkable.

★ **Casa Lleó Morera** (**D** B6)
→ Passeig de Gràcia, 35
The most sober of the three buildings that make up the *manzana de la discordia* ('block of discord') with Batlló and Amatller. The lobby and its Modernist staircase are worth seeing.

★ **Sagrada Família** (**D** D6)
*→ Carrer Mallorca, 401
Daily 9am–5.45pm (7.45pm March-Sep)*
Gaudí's exuberant masterpiece. The neogothic cathedral, still under construction, has become the symbol of the city. By 2022, the date set for the completion of the works, a total of 18 towers will stand over the sanctuary. Gaudí devoted his final 40 years (1883–1926) to this project. His body lies in the crypt. Two out of the three façades are visible: the much criticized 'Passion' has been entrusted to the sculptor Subirachs.

POBLE ESPANYOL

MUSEU NACIONAL
D'ART DE CATALUNYA

FOC
CARRER
DEL
CEMENTIRI
DEL
SUD-OEST
CAMÍ DEL MOLÍ
MIRADOR
5
CAMÍ DEL FAR
RONDA DEL LITORAL
RONDA
PASSEIG DE CANTUNIS
6
Moll Per a Petrolers
Moll del Sud
0 150 300 m
A
B

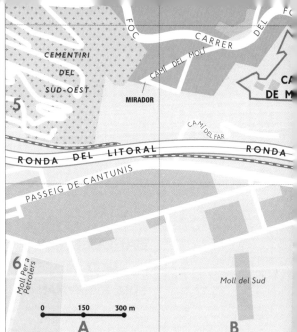

★ **CaixaForum** (**E** B2)
→ *Avinguda del Marquès de Comillas, 6–8*
Tel. 93 476 86 00
Mon-Sat 9am–8pm (10pm Sat)
There are no external clues as to the creativity and imagination that lurks behind these thick red-brick walls. The former Casarramona textile mill, designed by Puig i Cadafalch in 1913, now houses an Arts Center. Opened in July 2001, the center offers exhibitions, movies, talks and concerts.

★ **Font Màgica** (**E** B3)
→ *Plaça de Carles Buïgas, 1*
Son-et-lumière every half hour: Oct, Jan-April: Fri-Sat 7–9pm; May-Sep: Thu-Sun 8–11.30pm
A gigantic fountain built for the 1929 Exhibition, with changing water jets and son-et-lumière that impressed the entire world at the time. Restored in the 1950s, it is still a very kitsch attraction: the music of both Tchaikovsky and Abba has been used to accompany the dancing jets of water.

★ **Pavelló Mies van der Rohe** (**E** B3)
→ *Avinguda del Marquès de Comillas; Tel. 93 423 40 16*
Daily 10am–8pm
The first superb example of Modernist architecture in Barcelona, the German pavilion at the 1929 Universal Exhibition was designed by the leader of the Bauhaus movement. Demolished at the end of the event, this masterpiece was reconstructed almost on the same spot in 1986. Worth seeing, for the purity and sobriety of the lines.

★ **Poble Espanyol** (**E** B3)
→ *Avinguda del Marquès de Comillas; Tel. 93 508 63 00*
Daily 9am–2am (8pm Mon; 4am Fri-Sat; midnight Sun)
Entering Poble Espanyol is like seeing the whole of Spain in one go, with the entire range of architectural styles from the different regions represented. Entrance to the village is via the ramparts of Ávila; the main Castilian plaza leads to an Andalusian church and several typical Arago houses. The whole thing however, touristy and rat artificial, although the cra stores have a certain cha Very lively in the evening

★ **Museu Nacional d'Art de Catalunya (MNAC)** (**E** B3)
→ *Palau Nacional, Parc de Montjuïc; Tel. 93 622 03 75*
Tue-Sat 10am–7pm; Sun ar public hols 10am–2pm; www.mnac.es
One of the most beautifu medieval art museums ir the world, with some remarkable Roman and Gothic art, most notably frescos and altar shelves the former Museu d'Art d Catalunya was housed in

CAIXA FORUM

FONT MÀGICA

↑ Map C

A
B
1
2
3
MERCAT NOU
HOSTAFRANCS
MAGÓRIA LA CAMPANA
JARDINS DE L'ESPANYA INDUSTRIAL
C. DE LA CREU COBERTA
CARRER RIEGO
C. DE PREMIÀ
CARRER MASNOU
CARRER DE MUNTADAS
C. D'ERMENGARDA
C. DE LA RIERA TENA
C. DE BURGOS
C. DE SAGUNT
C. DE TOLEDO
C. DELS JOCS FLORALS
CARRER D'OLZINELLES
SANTA MARIA DE SANTS
C. DEL SANT CRIST
C. D'ALMERIA
C. DEL REI MARTÍ
CARRER ROSSEND ARÚS
CARRER DEL GUADIANA
Plaça de la Farga
CARRER DE GAIARRE
C. DEL VINT-I-SIS DE GENER 1641
C. DE MOIANÈS
C. DE LEIVA
C. DE L'ÀLIGA
C. DEL CONSELL
C. DEL RECTOR
C. DE LA CONSTITUCIÓ
C. DE GAVÀ
ST. ÀNGEL
CRA. DE LA BORDETA
C. DE MOSSÈN AMADEU OLLER
C. DE BARTOMEU
C. DEL CORRAL
C. DEL
C. DE SANT PERE D'ABANTO
C. DEL FARELL
Plaça de J. Corrades
GRAN VIA DE LES CORTS CATALANES
C. D'INDÍBIL
CARRER DE SANT FRUCTUÓS
CARRER FONT FLORIDA
C. DE LA GUATLLA
CARRER DE LA DÀLIA
C. DE MÈXIC
CAIXAFORUM ★
C. NORD
PAVELLÓ MIES VAN DER ROHE
CARRER DEL SEGURA
AV. DEL MARQUÈS DE COMILLAS
JOAN SERRAHIMA
Plaça de Sant Jordi
Plaça de C. Buïgas
Plaça del Pare Eusebi Millan
★ POBLE ESPANYOL
FONT MÀ
Plaça del Marquès de Fo
CAPELLA ROMÀNICA
PALAU D'ALFONS
PG. DE LES CASCAD
AVINGUDA DE L'ESTADI
MIRADOR DEL PALAU NACIONAL
TORRE CALATRAVA ★
Plaça d'Europa
PG. DE MINICI NATAL
★ MUSEU NAC. D'ART DE CATALUNYA
PISCINES BERNAT PICORNELL
C. DELS JOCS DEL 92
C. DE LA PEDRERA DEL MUSSOL
LES BANDERES
ANELLA OLÍMPICA
JARDINS DE JOAN MARAGALL
Plaça de Nemesi Ponsati
AVINGUDA DE L'ESTADI
PASSEIG DE
★ PALAU ST. JORDI
★ ESTADI OLÍMPIC
PASSEIG OLÍMPIC
C. DEL FOC
CTRA DEL FOMENT
CARRER DELS
CARRER DE

A city of hills, Barcelona designated that of Montjuïc to be the center of the 1992 Olympic Games. The infrastructure was developed by a team of the most brilliant designers, and today it is still the venue for major sports and leisure events, with superb walks along the coast.
Poble Sec, at the foot of Montjuïc, is the city's old theater area.
A 'moulin rouge' (now closed) aspired to be reminiscent of Paris' Montmartre, though the atmosphere in the area is now bohemian rather than cheeky. At Sant Antoni, bordering El Raval, restaurants and stores line the peaceful streets of this once working-class district.

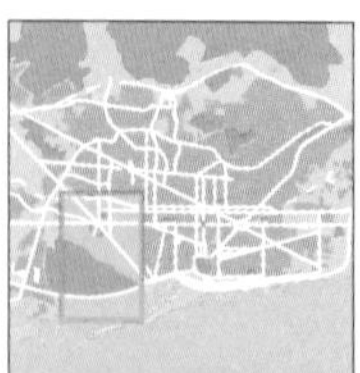

TAVERNA LA TOMAQUERA

SIRVENT

RESTAURANTS

Quimet & Quimet (**E** D4)
→ *Carrer Poeta Cabanyes, 25 Tel. 93 442 31 42*
Mon-Fri noon–4pm, 7–10.30pm; Sat noon–4pm
A narrow room with walls lined with bottles – mostly wine, some unknown, some famous and superb. Every day chef Quimet makes up many dozens of different *montaditos* (small rounds of toasted bread heaped with the day's ingredients), or you can have more classic tapas. A constant pleasure. Carte €13–17.

Dionisos (**E** D2)
→ *Carrer del Comte d'Urgell, 90; Tel. 93 451 54 17*
Daily 1.30–3.45pm, 8.30pm–midnight
Cretan wines and Greek specialties in a friendly, seaside-colored setting. Set lunch €8. Carte €22.

Taverna La Tomaquera (**E** C3)
→ *Carrer de Magallanes 58*
Tue-Sat 1.30–3.45pm, 8.30–10.45pm
Excellent grilled meats (with garlic mayonnaise, roquefort cheese or oil-and-vinegar dressing sauces), grilled quails, langoustines and snails, prettily laid out tables and a friendly owner-chef warrant the success of this place. Don't miss the sangria. Carte €20–25.

Elche (**E** D4)
→ *Carrer de Vila i Vilà, 71*
Tel. 93 441 30 89
Daily 1–4.30pm, 8pm–2am
Named after a town situated several miles from Alicante, this place serves paellas made with traditional recipes. Very friendly. Carte €28–30.

Restaurant de la Fundació Miró (**E** C4)
→ *Parc de Montjuïc*
Tel. 93 329 07 68; Tue-Sat 1–3.45pm (2pm Sun); Snack bar: same opening times as museum
With its luminous dining room with large bay windows that give onto the park and the huge terrace, this is a pleasant option for lunch on Montjuïc. Afternoon snacks available until 7pm. Dish of the day €12. Carte €23.

San Telmo (**E** D4)
→ *Carrer de Vila i Vilà, 53*
Tel. 93 441 30 78
Daily 1–4pm, 9pm–midnight (1am Sat-Sun)
Let the delicious smell of beef roasting on charcoal lead you to this place, a small and cosy restaurant, where Argentinian *churrasco* is served in an interior garden. The

TA ROJA

LA TERRRAZZA

CELLER FLORIDA

meats are imported, and portions can be huge. Let the staff proudly explain all the different cuts of beef, and enjoy. Carte €30.

Ca l'Isidre (**E** D4)
→ *Carrer les Flors, 12*
Tel. 93 441 11 39; Mon-Sat 1.30–3.30pm, 8.30–11pm
Tucked away between the Raval and Paral.lel, this restaurant is easy to miss. Those in the know, however (one of whom is said to be the King of Spain himself), are familiar with Ca l'Isidre's delicious Catalan fare. Always go for the dishes of the day. Carte €70.

CAFÉS

Sirvent (**E** D3)
→ *Carrer del Parlament, 56*
Tel. 93 441 27 20; Daily 9am–midnight (1.30am summer)
Most Barcelonese claim that for the past 85 years this café has served the finest *horchata*, and we believe them, but the ice cream and nougat are also scrumptious.

La Confiteria (**E** D4)
→ *Carrer de Sant Pau, 128 (corner of Ronda de St Pau)*
Mon-Fri 10am–3am; Sat-Sun noon–3am (midnight Sun)
A former patisserie converted into a café, where locals sit and chat over a coffee during the day. In the evening, however, the place turns into a lively bar where actors, stage crew and audience of the neighboring theaters come for an after-show drink.

BARS, CABARET, NIGHTCLUBS

Los Juanele (**E** D3)
→ *Carrer Aldana, 4; Tel. 616 29 44 22; Tue-Thu from 9pm; Fri-Sat 10.30pm–6am*
A friendly, authentic Andalusian flamenco club. Start with some tapas and a glass or two of wine before making for the dance floor to dance the *sevillanas*. Dance classes from 9–10pm on Thursday evenings.

Rouge (**E** D4)
→ *Carrer Poeta Cabanyes, 21*
Tel. 93 442 49 85
Thu-Sat 11pm–3.30am
With the look of a private club, this bar is one of the sexiest in the district: ring the bell of an unprepossessing door, enter, and cross the well-lit lobby with its red walls and comfortable sofas. Soul, jazz and lounge as ambient music, soft lights and expensive cocktails. Beware: on Sunday afternoons it sometimes becomes a meeting place for football supporters.

Tinta Roja (**E** C3)
→ *Carrer Creu dels Molers, 17; Tel. 93 443 32 43*
Thu-Sat 8pm–2am; Sun 7pm–12.30am
One of Barcelona's fairytale establishments, this is a traditional-style club, a long way from designer decor or electronic music. People come to soak up the atmosphere of this long-standing Argentinian cabaret club. Don't miss the tango displays at the weekend.

La Terrrazza / Discothèque (**E** B2)
→ *Avinguda del Marquès de Comillas, Poble Espanyol*
Tel. 93 423 12 85
Thu-Sat midnight–6am
The best place to hear house music in Barcelona, in the open air, in summer, surrounded by pine trees (La Terrrazza), or indoors (Discothèque) in winter. Drag queens, gogo dancers and bunny girls in abundance.

Sala Apolo (**E** D4)
→ *Carrer Nou de la Rambla, 113; Tel. 93 441 40 01*
Wed-Sat 12.30am–6.30am
A former ballroom, now a key venue for electronic music. Canibal Sound System (Afro-Cuban, ragga, reggae) on Wednesdays, Powder Room night (funk) on Thursdays.

SHOPPING

Mercat de Sant Antoni (**E** D3)
→ *Carrer del Comte d'Urgell, 1; Mon-Sat 7am–2.30pm, 5.30–8.30pm (non-stop Fri); Sun 9am–8pm*
Some say this market, designed in 1882 by Antoni Rovira i Trias, built from metal and glass and laid out in the shape of a Greek cross, is the most authentic building of its kind on the Rambles. Its iron shutters open onto colorful shops selling fresh produce and clothing, and, on Sundays, books, coins, comics, postcards etc. Good value and less known, therefore less touristy than La Boqueria.

Celler Florida (**E** D2)
→ *Carrer Floridablanca, 112*
Tel. 93 325 86 04
Tue-Fri 10am–2pm, 5–9pm; Sat 10am–3pm, 5.30–9pm; Sun 11am–2.30pm
Cavas and Spanish wines are sold retail or by the liter – you can fill your own bottle from the barrel (tasting permitted). The owner will be happy to help.

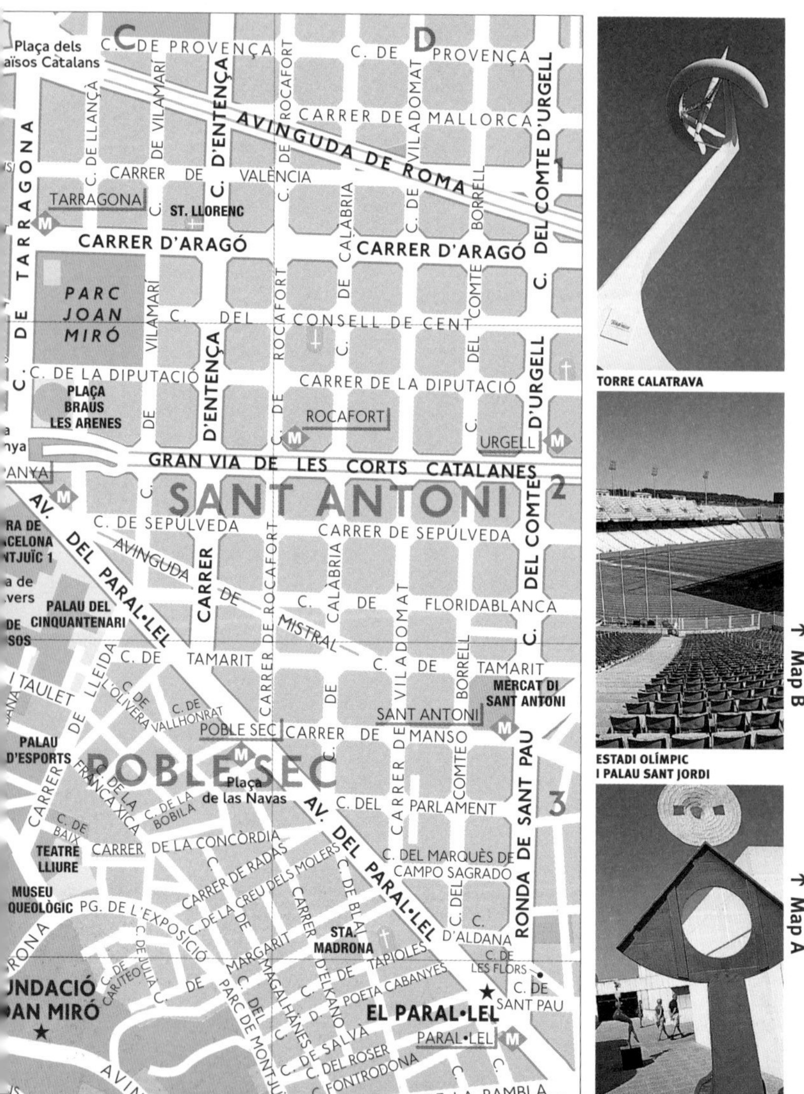

TORRE CALATRAVA

ESTADI OLÍMPIC I PALAU SANT JORDI

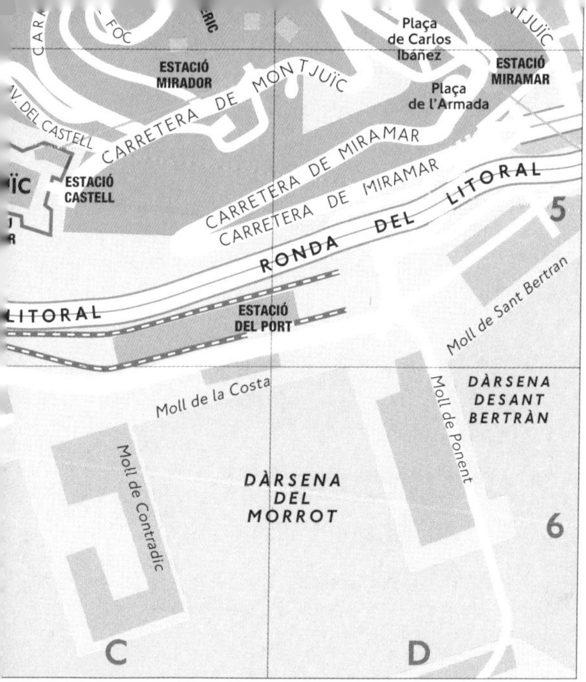

CASTELL DE MONTJUÏC

EL PARAL.LEL

: main building of the
29 Exhibition since 1934.
1990, the MNAC was
eated, adding to the
sting collections those of
Museu d'Art Modern
th- and 20th-century
talan art), and now also
lude decorative arts and
otography.

Estadi Olímpic (**E** B4)/
alau Sant Jordi (**E** A4)
Passeig Olímpic, 17–19
d 5–7; Tel. 93 426 20 89
using some 55,000
ectators in the stadium
d 17,000 in the sports
vilion or *palau*, the
ectacular infrastructures
ilt to house the 1992
mpic Games still host
city's major events.

Designed by the Japanese architect Arata Isozaki, the *palau* is seen as a symbol of the modernity of the new Montjuïc district.

★ **Torre Calatrava** (**E** A3)
→ *Plaça Europa*
Easily identifiable from a distance, due to its unusual shape, the telecommunication tower was designed by the architect Calatrava in 1992. It is also constructed to work as a sundial, the spire's shadow being thrown onto its circular base, which is graduated to indicate the hour of the day.

★ **Fundació Joan Miró** (**E** C4)
→ *Parc de Montjuïc*
Tel. 93 443 94 70
Tue-Sat 10am–7pm (8pm summer; 9.30pm Thu); Sun 10am–2.30pm; http://fundaciomiro-bcn.org
Miró was over 80 when the foundation that bears his name opened in 1975. Superbly organized, it contains the best of the Catalan master's art, with over 10,000 works.

★ **Castell de Montjuïc** (**E** B5)
→ *Parc de Montjuïc*
Tel. 93 329 86 13; Tue-Sun 9.30am–6.30pm (7pm Sat-Sun). April-Sep: daily 9am–7pm (8pm Sat-Sun)
Built in the 13th century, the castle served as a military prison (a torture center during the Franco dictatorship) and was associated with political repression until it was handed over to the city in 1960. Today it houses a military museum (collection of ancient weapons, maps and models). There are magnificent views over the city from the castle ramparts.

★ **El Paral.lel** (**E** D4)
→ *Around Av. del Paral.lel*
The theaters, cabarets and music halls have all gone in this former industrial area, whose lively nightlife attracted people from the city center until the 1950s. Only three huge chimneys remain of what was a power station, now a park popular with rollerbladers.

SERRE TROPICALE

PARC DE LA CIUTADELLA

AV. MARQUÈS DE L'ARGENTERA
MODERN
CARRER
DEL
ESTACIÓ DE FRANÇA
PASSEIG DE CIRCUMVAL·LACIÓ
PARC ZOOLÒGIC
CARRER
PARC CARLES I
MOSCOU
BARCELONETA
CIUTADELLA VILA OLÍMPICA
C. DE RAMON T. FARGAS
CARRER DE
A
CARRER DEL DOCTOR AIGUADER
RONDA DEL LITORAL
CARRER
5
C. DE BALBOA
CARRER DE GINEBRA
C. DE LA MAQUINISTA
C. D'ANDREA DÒRIA
C. DE SANT CARLES
PG. DE SALVAT PAPASSEIT
CARRER Plaça dels Voluntaris Olímpics
DE
PARC DE LES CASCADES
CARRER DEL DOCTOR AIGUADER
LA BARCELONETA
Plaça de la Font
HOSPITAL DEL MAR
PARC DE LA BARCELONETA
PASSEIG MARÍTIM DE LA BARCELONETA
Platja de la Barceloneta
6
0 150 300 m
A
B

★ Teatre Nacional de Catalunya i l'Auditori (**F** C3)
→ *Plaça de les Arts, 1*
Tel. 93 306 57 55 (theater);
Carrer Lepant, 150
Tel. 93 247 93 00 (auditorium)
In 1997, the Catalan Ricardo Bofill designed a theater whose grandiose silhouette was reminiscent of the Parthenon. The auditorium next door was opened in 1999: Moneo, from Madrid, was the designer of this new building with its state-of-the-art technology and extraordinary acoustics. The recent renovation of the district around the Plaça de les Glòries Catalanes completes, some 150 years later, the original vision of the engineer Cerdà (author of the Eixample town planning project), who saw it as the city's new center.

★ Parc del Estació del Nord (**F** B3)
→ *Avinguda de Vilanova*
Daily 10am–6pm (7pm March and Oct; 8pm April and Sep; 9pm May-Aug)
The most unusual park in Barcelona opened in 1988 behind the disused North Station. The sculptures by Beverly Pepper, in blue and white mosaic, are inspired by Gaudí. Strewn around the lawns, they brighten the park here and there, appearing by benches and behind trees.

★ Arc de Triomf (**F** A3)
→ *Passeig de Lluís Companys*
In 1888, the architect Vilaseca was asked to design a landmark that would symbolize the Universal Exhibition. He decided upon the classical theme of a triumphant arch and built the monumental arch using simple brick, to reflect the fashion at the time for neo-Mudéjar style.

★ Museus i Zoo del Parc de la Ciutadella (**F** A4)
→ *Corner of Passeig de Pujades/Passeig de Picasso*
Tel. 93 225 67 80 (zoo); 933 196 912 (museum); daily 10am–9pm (zoo)
For a short cultural stopc visit the Citadel park. He you are spoilt for choice: geological museum, zoological museum, two greenhouses and a zoo. of these are housed eith in splendid pavilions fro the 1888 Universal Exhibition or former milit buildings.

★ Parc de la Ciutadella (**F** A4)
→ *Corner of Passeig de Pujades/Passeig de Picass Daily 10am–6pm (7pm Ma and Oct; 8pm April and Se 9pm May-Aug)*
Once the site of the 1888 Exhibition, and formerly

↑ Map D

TEATRE NACIONAL DE CATALUNYA I L'AUDITORI

PARC DE L'ESTACIÓ DEL NORD

A
B
1
2
3

JARDINS DE CATERINA ALBERT
C. DEL ROSSELLÓ
C. DEL ROSSELLÓ
VERDAGUER
SAGRADA FAMÍLIA
CARRER DE PROVENÇA
AVINGUDA DIAGONAL
Plaça de la Sagrada Família
SAGRADA FAMÍLIA
Plaça Mossèn Jacint Verdaguer
CARRER DE VALÈNCIA
CARRER D'ARAGÓ
Plaça de Pablo Neruda
CARRER DEL CONSELL DE CENT
GIRONA
CARRER DE LA DIPUTACIÓ
TETUAN
Plaça de Tetuan
GRAN VIA DE LES CORTS CATALANES
Plaça Braus Monumental
EL FORT PIUS
CARRER DE CASP
C. D'AUSIÀS MARC
RONDA DE ST. PERE
C. D'ALÍ BEI
CARRER DE RIBES
C. DE TRAFALGAR
Plaça de Sant Pere
ARC DE TRIOMF
ESTACIÓ DEL NORD
AV. DE VILANOVA
★ ARC DE TRIOMF
★ L'ESTACIÓ DEL NORD
PARC DE L'ESTACIÓ DEL NORD
C. DEL REC COMTAL
C. DE ST. PERE MÉS BAIX
LA RIBERA
C. DELS ALMOGÀVERS
PALAU DE JUSTICIA
C. DE BUENAVENTURA MUÑOZ
AV. MERIDIANA
Plaça de St. A. Vell
C. DE CALDERS
PG. DE PUJADES
C. DE PUJADES
PG. DE J. RENART
★ MUSEUS I ZOO
C. DE LA PRINCESA
METRÒNOM
C. DEL BRUC
C. DE GIRONA
CARRER DE BAILÈN
PTGE. DEL MERCAT
PG. DE ST. JOAN
PASSEIG DE SANT JOAN
C. DE ROGER DE FLOR
C. DE NÀPOLS
C. DE SICÍLIA
CARRER DE SARDENYA
CARRER DE LA MARINA
PASSEIG DE LLUÍS COMPANYS
PICASSO
COMERÇ

↑ Map B

Even the people of Barcelona seem scarcely able to believe that before 1992 the coastal area of the city was nothing but a vast wasteland. Today it is a mystery how the city ever survived without its beaches, new parks and shopping centers filled with restaurants, bars and trendy nightclubs. Functional and modern, the transformations have resulted in the revival of the Poblenou area; the former factories have been turned into artists' studios, and the lively nightlife is in full swing seven nights a week. The Dreta area, more residential in tone, is worth a detour, if only for its flea market.

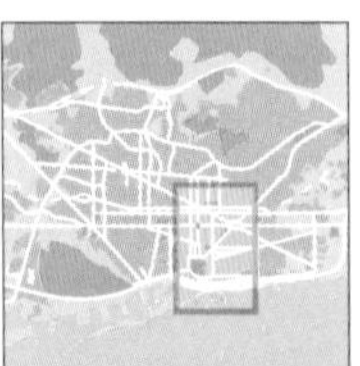

CAN RAMONET

AGUA

RESTAURANTS

El Vaso de Oro (**F** A5)
→ *Carrer de Balboa, 6*
Tel. 93 319 30 98
Daily 9am (noon Sat-Sun)–midnight
This small place is almost always busy, mostly packed with locals who adore the tapas of the day. Excellent Catalan beer too. Carte €10–20.

Els Pollos de Llull (**F** C4)
→ *Carrer de Ramon Turró, 13; Tel. 93 221 32 06*
Daily 1pm–1am
Good quality dishes at reasonable prices (the weekday lunch menu is only €6) are served in a huge dining room resembling a warehouse with basic facilities. The grilled chicken, fries and salads are popular with families returning from the beach or from a visit of the nearby zoo. Carte €12.

San Fermín (**F** C6)
→ *Moll de Gregal, 22*
Tel. 93 221 02 09
Daily 1pm–midnight
If, despite (or perhaps because of) the dozens of restaurants squeezed along the quayside of Port Olímpic, you can't decide where to go for a good night out, this Basque cider-works is a good bet. Roasted meat and sausages, chorizo cooked in cider, unlimited beer and cider. Set menu €29.

Xiringuito Escribà (**F** D5)
→ *Ronda del litoral, 42*
Tel. 93 221 07 29
Daily 10am–6pm (and Fri-Sat 9pm–1am in summer; kitchen 1–4.30pm
A greasy spoon (*xiringuito*) café located in front of the Bogatell beach. Paella and grilled seafood are prepared in front of you by an army of energetic cooks and served on the large wooden terrace. Salads and the usual tapas – tuna croquettes, *patatas bravas*, marinated anchovies on a slice of *pà amb tomaquet* – are also available. Carte €30.

Can Ramonet (**F** A5)
→ *Carrer de la Maquinista, 17 Tel. 93 319 30 64*
Daily 1pm–1am
One of the oldest eateries in the harbor zone (1763), this former dockers' bodega is now one of the best restaurants in the city, serving top-quality cuisine based on fish and seafood (oysters, grilled razor-clams, scallops in cava), and a variety of tapas (dry meats, duck ham and asparagus).

N SOLÉ

PORT OLÍMPIC

ENCANTS VELLS

Inviting terrace on the small square, near the Barceloneta market. Carte €30–36 .

Agua (**F** B5)
→ *Passeig Marítim de la Barceloneta, 30*
Tel. 93 225 12 72
Mon-Fri 1–3.15pm, 8–11.30pm (12.30am Fri); Sat-Sun 1–4.30pm, 8pm–12.30am (11.30pm Sun)
A few yards from the extremely modern Port Olímpic, this colonial-style restaurant opens right onto the beach. Delicious fish and seafood dishes. Carte €30–35.

Restaurante Can Solé (**F** A6)
→ *Carrer Sant Carles, 4*
Tel. 93 221 50 12
Tue-Sat 1–4pm, 8.30–11.30pm; Sun 1–4pm
Set apart from the touristic street that runs along the seafront, 'Can Solé' is a classic on Barcelona's gastronomic map, popular with residents and therefore a reliable choice. Excellent seafood and rice dishes (allow 20 minutes cooking for the latter). Carte € 42.

CAFÉ, TAPAS

El Tío Ché (**F** D4)
→ *Rambla del Poblenou, 44-46; Tel. 93 309 18 72*
Mon-Tue, Thu-Sun 10am–2pm, 5–10pm (daily 10am–2am in summer)
On Barcelona's other main boulevard, where the city still has the feel of a market town, food-lovers meet up at 'Uncle Ché' to drink a *granizat*, *horchata* or milk shake, eat an ice cream or a chunk of homemade nougat.

Princesa 23 (**F** A4)
→ *Carrer de la Princesa, 23*
Tel. 93 319 04 72
Daily noon–3am (kitchen noon–11pm)
Legend has it that this bar once housed the confessionals from the church next door. Enticing cocktails at reasonable prices and creative Catalan cuisine.

THEATER, BARS, NIGHTCLUBS

Casino L'Aliança del Poblenou (**F** D4)
→ *Rambla del Poblenou, 42*
Tel. 93 225 28 14
www.casinoalianca.com
Keep an eye on the varied program of this former theater: its list of performers is likely to include anything from the Sari Gül dancing dervishes to the local brass band.

Megataverna L'Ovella Negra (**F** C4)
→ *Carrer Zamora, 78*
Tel. 93 309 59 38 ; Thu 10pm–2.30am; Fri-Sun 5pm–3am (10.30pm Sun)
A bar with long wooden tables and a lively ambience – where a youngish crowd gathers for a beer or sangria in the early part of the evening.

Razzmatazz (**F** C3)
→ *Carrer Almogàvers, 122*
Tel. 93 320 82 00
Fri-Sat and eves of public hols 1–5am
Razzmatazz is an old concert hall that has been converted into a huge space dedicated to alternative culture: concerts, exhibitions, fashion shows... At the weekend that space is divided into a series of clubs that will delight music aficionados: for example there's indie pop rock at the Razz Club, gothic at the Temple Beat, pop and 1960s at the Pop Bar, house and electro at the Loft, and more.

Port Olímpic (**F** B-C5)
A very animated place at night, the promenade is bordered with palm trees, cafés and numerous nightclubs, most of which will let you in for free, so hop in and out until you find what you're looking for: salsa, techno, pop...

SHOPPING

Els encants Vells: flea market (**F** C2)
→ *Carrer del Dos de Maig, 186; Mon, Wed, Fri-Sat 9am–6pm*
Venture here for an amazing range of bric-à-brac, with rumba music playing in the background. It's a little confusing, with the most surprising items seeming to appear out of nowhere just when you least expect them. To give you a head start: hats, dress-jewelry and other baubles on stand 15; 1960s furniture on stands 103–104; 1970s fashion-wear on stands 106–111 and psychedelic colors and retro clothing on stands 112–120.

Mango Outlet (**F** A2)
→ *Carrer de Girona, 37*
Tel. 93 412 29 35
Mon-Sat 10.15pm–9pm
Last year's collections by the Spanish brand Mango at incredible prices (between 20 and 50 percent discount). Be prepared to rummage through huge trays to find handbags, T-shirts and shoes.

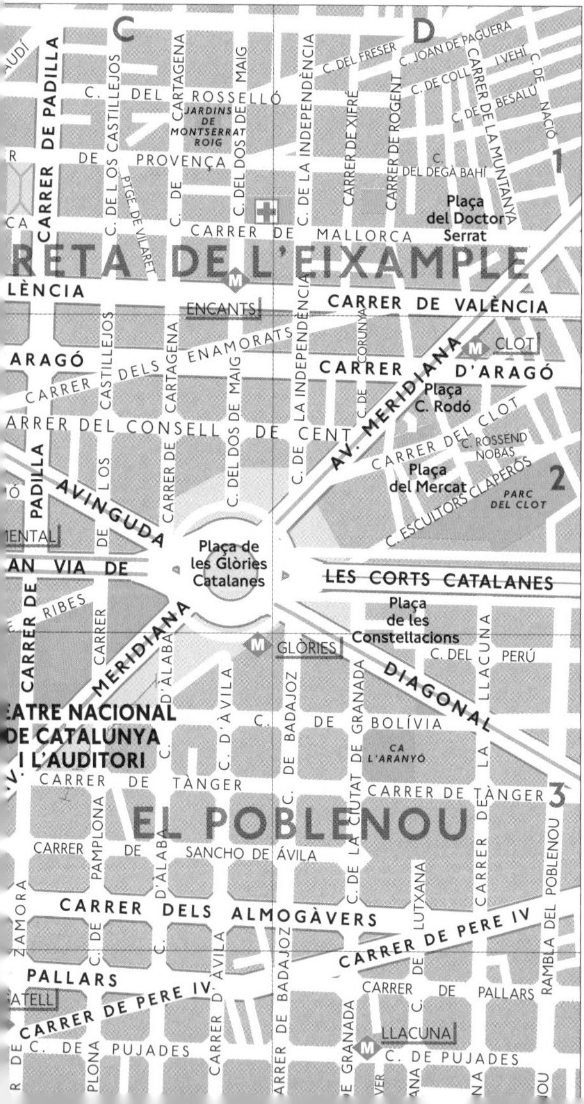

C
D
1
2
3

RETA DE L'EIXAMPLE

EL POBLENOU

C. DEL ROSSELLÓ
JARDINS DE MONTSERRAT ROIG
DE PROVENÇA
CARRER DE MALLORCA
Plaça del Doctor Serrat
LÈNCIA
CARRER DE VALÈNCIA
ENCANTS
ARAGÓ
CARRER D'ARAGÓ
CARRER DELS ENAMORATS
CLOT
Plaça C. Rodó
CARRER DEL CONSELL DE CENT
AV. MERIDIANA
CARRER DEL CLOT
C. ROSSEND NOBAS
Plaça del Mercat
C. ESCULTORS CLAPERÓS
PARC DEL CLOT
AVINGUDA
MENTAL
Plaça de les Glòries Catalanes
AN VIA DE
LES CORTS CATALANES
Plaça de les Constellacions
GLÒRIES
C. DEL PERÚ
MERIDIANA
DIAGONAL
EATRE NACIONAL DE CATALUNYA I L'AUDITORI
C. DE BOLÍVIA
CA L'ARANYÓ
CARRER DE TÀNGER
CARRER DE SANCHO DE ÁVILA
CARRER DELS ALMOGÀVERS
CARRER DE PERE IV
PALLARS
CARRER DE PALLARS
ATELL
LLACUNA
C. DE PUJADES
CARRER DE PADILLA
C. DE LOS CASTILLEJOS
CARTAGENA
C. DEL DOS DE MAIG
C. DE LA INDEPENDÈNCIA
CARRER DE XIFRÉ
CARRER DE ROGENT
C. DEL FRESER
C. JOAN DE PAGUERA
C. DE COLL I VEHÍ
CARRER DE LA MUNTANYA
C. DE BESALÚ
C. DE NACIÓ
C. DEL DEGÀ BAHÍ
PTGE. DE VILARET
CORUNYA
CARRER DE RIBES
C. D'ÀLABA
C. D'ÀVILA
C. DE BADAJOZ
C. DE LA CIUTAT DE GRANADA
CARRER DE LA LLACUNA
CARRER DE PAMPLONA
ZAMORA
C. DE LUTXANA
RAMBLA DEL POBLENOU

MUSEUS I ZOO DEL PARC DE LA CIUTADELLA

DIPÒSIT DE LES AIGÜES

VILA OLÍMPICA

PORT OLÍMPIC

ıitary citadel, this has come the green lung of e city (42 acres). It has a onumental waterfall, ne of Barcelona's best-own sculptures and a ating lake. A real oasis ay from the bustle of the city, it is particularly pular on Sundays.

Dipòsit les Aigües (**F** B4)
Carrer de Ramon Trías gas, 25–27
93 542 17 09; Mon-Fri m–1.30pm; Sat-Sun and blic hols 10am–9pm
s hidden gem is well rth the effort it takes to d it. Adjoining the Citadel k, the water tower (1888), unknown by the majority of tourists, has been magnificently restored and converted into a university library. Behind a somewhat insignificant red-brick façade is a staggering maze of 46 foot-tall pillars.

★ **El Poblenou** (**F** D4)
→ *Around La Rambla del Poblenou*
Once one of the poorer areas of the city, Poblenou has benefited from the seafront renovations for the 1992 Olympic games. This workers' district was once known as the 'Catalan Manchester', but is today home to many artists, who have transformed the old factory premises into exciting studios and workshops (open days take place in early June). Don't hesitate to climb the perpendicular streets to La Rambla del Poblenou, a thoroughfare planted to resemble Provençal promenades.

★ **Port Olímpic / Vila Olímpica** (**F** C5)
→ *Ciutadella Vila Olímpica subway station*
This is an extraordinary example of urban redevelopment. The reshaping of the old industrial seafront for the 1992 Olympic Games has given the city an area entirely devoted to sport and leisure. The Olympic village has today been reconverted into a residential zone with 2,000 apartments. Where previously the dilapidated dockside buildings masked the view of the sea there are now some 2 ½ miles of beach, with restaurants, bars, and extraordinarily avant-garde architecture. As a symbol of this urban renaissance, is the golden fish by Frank Gehry (1992), surrounded by the city's first two sky-scrapers: the 500-foot high Arts and the 515-foot high Mapfre towers.

TMB
R4 Sant Vicenç de Calders
T3 Consell Comarcal
Torreblanca
Walden
Rambla de Sant Just
T2 Sant Martí de l'Erm
Sant Martí de l'Erm
A-2 (Lleida-Tarragona)
T1 Bon Viatge
La Fontsanta
S33 Can Ros
S4 Olesa de Montserrat
S8 Martorell-Enllaç
R5 Manresa-Baixador
R6 Igualada
Fontsanta Fatjó
Centre Miquel Martí i Pol
La Sardana
Pont d'Esplugues
Montesa
Can Clota
Les Aigües
El Pedró
Ignasi Iglésias
Cornellà
Cornellà
Ca n'Oliveres
Can Rigal
L5
Cornellà Centre
L8
Molí Nou-Ciutat Cooperativa
Sant Boi
Cornellà-Riera
Gavarra
Ctra de l'Hospitalet
Sant Ildefons
Can Boixeres
Can Vidalet
Pubilla Cases
l'Hospitalet de Llobregat
Can Serra
Florida
Almeda
Cornellà de Llobregat
R1 R3 R4 R7
Rbla Just Oliveras
l'Hospitalet - Av Carrilet
Av Carrilet
l'Hospitalet de Llobregat
Riu Llobregat
St. Josep
Bellvitge
Bellvitge
Gornal
L1
Hospital de Bellvitge
R2 Sant Vicenç de Calders
Autovia de Castelldefels
El Prat de Llobregat
R10 Aeroport
Europa Fira
Ildefons Cerdà
Magòria La Campana
Fira 2
Pg Zona Franca
Zona Universitària
Av de Xile
St. Ramon
Palau Reial
Palau Reial
Pius XII
Maria Cristina
Maria Cristina
Numància
L'Illa
L3 Av Esplugues
Zona Universitària
Collblanc
Torrassa
Badal
Santa Eulàlia
Mercat Nou
Plaça de Sants
Riera Blanca
Trav de les Corts
Av Madrid
Les Corts
Plaça del Centre
Gran Via Carles III
Av Joan XXIII
Estadi F.C. Barcelona
Barcelona-Sants
Sants Estació
Parc de l'Espanya Industrial
Hostafrancs
Tarragona
Parc de Joan Miró
Rda del Mig
Pl Ildefons Cerdà
Gran Via
Espanya
L8 Espanya
S33 S4 S8
R5 R6
Av Paral·lel
Rocafort
Urgell
Sant Antoni
Poble Sec
Anella Olímpica
Palau Nacional
Fundació Miró
L2
Paral·lel
Parc de Montjuïc
Paral·lel
Parc de Montjuïc
Castell de Montjuïc
Telefèric de Montjuïc
Mirador
Miramar
Jaume I
T1 T2 T3
Francesc Macià
Entença
Hospital Clínic
Av Roma
Comte d'Urgell
Les Planes
S5
S55
S2
S1
Baixador de Vallvidrera
Túnel de Vallvidrera
Peu del Funicular
Parc de l'Oreneta
Ronda de Dalt
Major de Sarrià
L6
Reina Elisenda
Pg Reina Elisenda
Hospital Sant Joan de Déu
Av Tibidabo
Sarrià
Pg Sant Joan Bosco
Codi Código Key
Estació d'autobusos Estación de autobuses Bus station
Estació Marítima Estación Marítima Seaboard station
Tramvia Blau Tranvía azul Blue tram
Funicular Funicular Funicular railway
Telefèric Teleférico Cable-car
Centres d'atenció al client Centros atención clientes Customers service centres
Estació Estación Station
Estació terminal Estación terminal Terminus station
Estació de correspondència Estación de correspondencia Connecting station
L1 Hospital de Bellvitge, Bellvitge, Av Carrilet, Can Serra, Florida, Santa Eulàlia, Hostafrancs, Rocafort, Urgell, Universitat, Marina, Glòries, Sagrera, Fabra i Puig, Sant Andreu, Torras i Bages, Trinitat Vella, Baró de Viver
L2 Totes les estacions Todas las estaciones All stations
L3 Plaça del Centre, Sants-Estació, ParaHel, Catalunya, Mundet, Valldaura, Canyelles
L5 Cornellà Centre, Sant Ildefons, Can Boixeres, Pubilla Cases, Badal, Hospital de Sant Pau
L6 Catalunya, Provença, Muntaner, La Bonanova, Les Tres Torres, Reina Elisenda, Baixador de Vallvidrera, Les Planes
L7 Catalunya, Provença, Av Tibidabo
L8 Espanya, Magòria-La Campana, L'Hospitalet-Av Carrilet, Cornellà-Riera, Sant Boi, Molí Nou-Ciutat Cooperativa, Europa | Fira, Almeda
L11 Totes les estacions Todas las estaciones All stations
Totes les estacions Todas las estaciones All stations
L1 Catalunya
L3 Drassanes, Liceu, Fontana
L4 La Pau, Besòs, Besòs Mar, El Maresme Fòrum, Passeig de Gràcia, Joanic, Alfons X, Llucmajor, Via Júlia, Trinitat Nova
L5 Gavarra, Sants Estació, Entença, Hospital Clínic, Camp de l'Arpa, Sagrera, Congrés, Vilapicina
L6 Sant Gervasi
Plaça Catalunya, Barcelona-Sants
Peu del Funicular

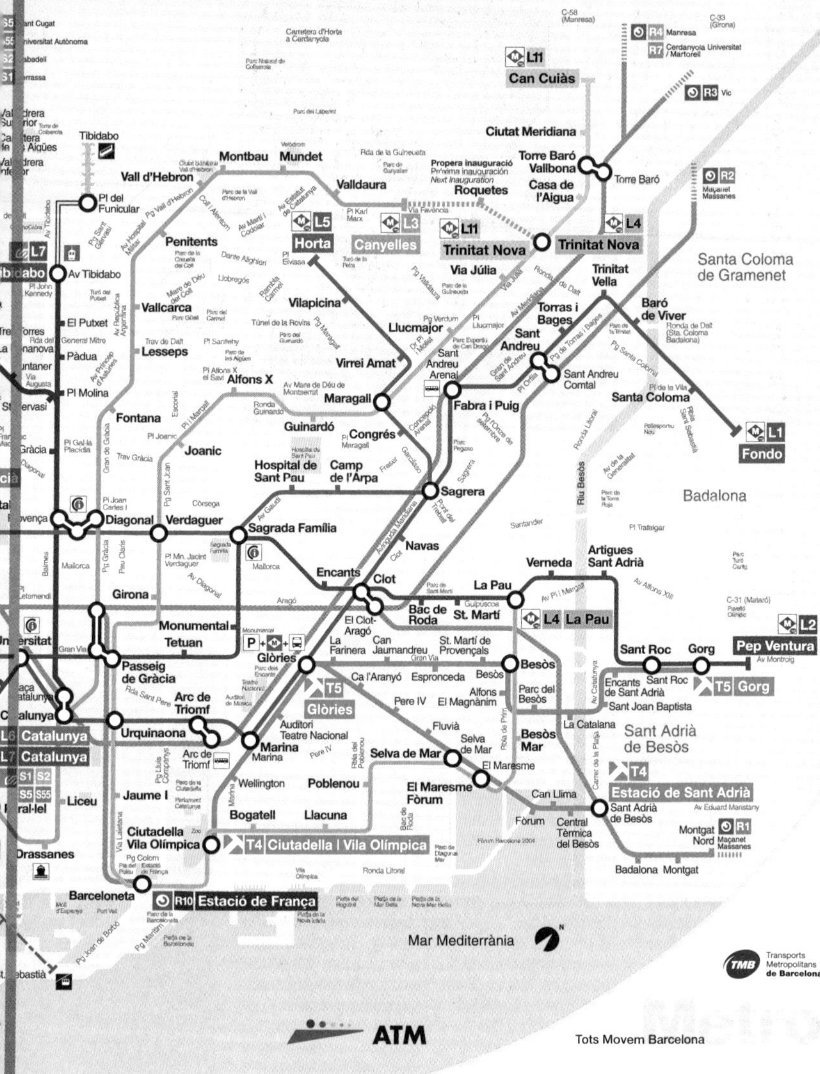

S5 Sant Cugat
S55 Universitat Autònoma
S2 Sabadell
S1 Terrassa
C-58 (Manresa)
C-33 (Girona)
R4 Manresa
R7 Cerdanyola Universitat / Martorell
R3 Vic
L11 Can Cuiàs
Carretera d'Horta a Cerdanyola
Tibidabo
Vallvidrera Superior
Carretera de les Aigües
Vallvidrera Inferior
Ciutat Meridiana
Torre Baró Vallbona
Torre Baró
Montbau
Mundet
Vall d'Hebron
Valldaura
Propera inauguració
Pròxima inauguración
Next Inauguration
Roquetes
Casa de l'Aigua
R2 Maçanet Massanes
Pl del Funicular
L5 Horta
L3 Canyelles
L11 Trinitat Nova
L4 Trinitat Nova
Penitents
Santa Coloma de Gramenet
L7 Tibidabo
Av Tibidabo
Via Júlia
Trinitat Vella
Vallcarca
Vilapicina
Torras i Bages
Baró de Viver
El Putxet
Llucmajor
Sant Andreu
Lesseps
Pàdua
Virrei Amat
Sant Andreu Arenal
Sant Andreu Comtal
Pl Molina
Alfons X
Maragall
Fabra i Puig
Santa Coloma
Fontana
Guinardó
Congrés
L1 Fondo
Joanic
Hospital de Sant Pau
Camp de l'Arpa
Sagrera
Badalona
Provença
Diagonal
Verdaguer
Sagrada Família
Navas
Encants
Clot
Verneda
Artigues Sant Adrià
La Pau
Girona
Bac de Roda
St. Martí
L4 La Pau
El Clot-Aragó
Monumental
Tetuan
L2 Pep Ventura
Universitat
La Farinera
Can Jaumandreu
St. Martí de Provençals
Sant Roc
Gorg
Glòries
Besòs
Passeig de Gràcia
Ca l'Aranyó
Espronceda
T5 Glòries
T5 Gorg
Alfons El Magnànim
Parc del Besòs
Encants de Sant Adrià
Sant Joan Baptista
Arc de Triomf
Pere IV
La Catalana
Sant Adrià de Besòs
Catalunya
Urquinaona
Fluvià
Besòs Mar
L6 Catalunya
L7 Catalunya
Marina
Auditori Teatre Nacional
Selva de Mar
El Maresme
T4 Estació de Sant Adrià
Wellington
Poblenou
El Maresme Fòrum
Can Llima
Liceu
Jaume I
Bogatell
Llacuna
Fòrum
Central Tèrmica del Besòs
Sant Adrià de Besòs
Montgat Nord
R1 Maçanet Massanes
Ciutadella Vila Olímpica
T4 Ciutadella | Vila Olímpica
Drassanes
Paral·lel
Badalona
Montgat
Barceloneta
R10 Estació de França
Ronda Litoral
Mar Mediterrània
St. Sebastià
TMB Transports Metropolitans de Barcelona
ATM
Tots Movem Barcelona

Street names, monuments and places to visit are listed alphabetically. They are followed by a map reference, of which the initial letter(s) in bold (**A, B, C**...) relate to the matching map(s) within this guide.

Streets